本书由西安翻译学院资助出版（项目编号：JC20B04）

英译教程

A Coursebook on Chinese Culture Translation

罗 飞 焦艳伟 张 睿 主编

西安交通大学出版社
XI'AN JIAOTONG UNIVERSITY PRESS
国家一级出版社
全国百佳图书出版单位

图书在版编目(CIP)数据

中国文化英译教程 / 罗飞,焦艳伟,张睿主编. —
西安:西安交通大学出版社,2022.9
ISBN 978-7-5693-2570-6

Ⅰ.①中… Ⅱ.①罗… ②焦… ③张… Ⅲ.①中华文
化-英语-翻译-教材 Ⅳ.①G122

中国版本图书馆 CIP 数据核字(2022)第 069479 号

中国文化英译教程
ZHONGGUO WENHUA YINGYI JIAOCHENG

主　　编	罗　飞　焦艳伟　张　睿
责任编辑	牛瑞鑫
责任校对	张静静

出版发行	西安交通大学出版社
	(西安市兴庆南路 1 号　邮政编码 710048)
网　　址	http://www.xjtupress.com
电　　话	(029)82668357　82667874(市场营销中心)
	(029)82668315(总编办)
传　　真	(029)82668280
印　　刷	陕西日报印务有限公司
开　　本	720 mm×1000 mm　1/16　印张 10　字数 200 千字
版次印次	2022 年 9 月第 1 版　2022 年 9 月第 1 次印刷
书　　号	ISBN 978-7-5693-2570-6
定　　价	49.80 元

如发现印装质量问题,请与本社市场营销中心联系。
订购热线:(029)82665248　(029)82667874

版权所有　侵权必究

前言

随着中国国际地位的逐步提高,推动中国文化"走出去"已然成为时代发展的需要。中国文化外译活动空前繁荣,进入了一个新的历史发展阶段。

因此中国文化英译在翻译教学中具有十分重要的地位和作用。课程相关主讲教师经过两年的前期准备,将翻译实践与翻译理论有机结合,在课程上通过大量实践练习,帮助学生内化翻译理论,强化翻译实践,培养学生敏锐的原文分析能力、灵活的译文转换能力、翻译过程中的自我监控能力、使用翻译策略的能力、跨文化交际能力、中国文化传播意识及读者认知关注能力。

该教材紧扣时代发展对文化翻译人才的需求,积极响应中国文化"走出去"战略,系统融合了理论与实践。本教材适合英语翻译专业使用,选取内容涵盖翻译理论与实践两大模块,内容丰富、题材鲜明、难易适度、实用性强。本教材最大的特色在于通过大量实践及案例分析,引导学生举一反三地展开翻译实践活动,能够更加有效地培养学生跨语言及跨文化翻译能力。

本教材旨在助力打造完整的翻译专业学科体系,全面促进学生语言技能、学科素养、文化素养和创新能力的提升。

本教材关注学生语言基本功的训练,扩充学生中外语言文化知识与相关百科知识,突出对各类知识的传授和积累,注重培养学生对中外文化差异的理解和包容,加强学生的翻译思辨能力、创新意识和实践能力,锻炼学生自主学习能力,特别是网络环境下的自主学习能力。

本教材共20万字,其中罗飞编写10万字,焦艳伟编写10万字,张睿负责全书审定。本教材为西安翻译学院2020年度校级教材建设项目(项目编号:JC20B04)。同时,本教材也是2021年西安翻译学院高级翻译学院陕西省虚拟教研室阶段性成果和2022年度陕西高校青年创新团队"中华优秀文化翻译与国际传播创新团队"阶段性成果。

目 录
CONTENTS

理论篇

第一章　翻译概述 ………………………………………… 3
　　1. 翻译的性质 ………………………………………… 3
　　2. 翻译单位 …………………………………………… 4
　　3. 翻译过程 …………………………………………… 5
　　4. 译者的素养 ………………………………………… 15
　　练习题 ………………………………………………… 16

第二章　英汉语言对比 …………………………………… 19
　　1. 英汉语义对比 ……………………………………… 19
　　2. 句法结构对比 ……………………………………… 21
　　练习题 ………………………………………………… 24

第三章　翻译与文化 ……………………………………… 25
　　1. 文化趋同与语言的融合 …………………………… 25
　　2. 文化差异与翻译 …………………………………… 27
　　3. 心理文化与翻译 …………………………………… 32
　　练习题 ………………………………………………… 41

第四章　专有名词的翻译 ………………………………… 43
　　1. 人名翻译 …………………………………………… 43
　　2. 地名翻译 …………………………………………… 44
　　3. 文化术语翻译 ……………………………………… 45
　　练习题 ………………………………………………… 48

第五章　习语与翻译 · 49

1. 汉语成语的翻译 · 49
2. 汉语歇后语的翻译 · 56
3. 汉语谚语的翻译 · 61

练习题 · 64

第六章　汉语委婉语的文化内涵与翻译 · 67

1. 委婉语的语言功能 · 67
2. 汉语委婉语的特征 · 69
3. 汉语委婉语的翻译 · 71

练习题 · 74

第七章　汉语颜色词的文化内涵与翻译 · 75

1. 汉语颜色词的分类 · 75
2. 汉语颜色词的文化内涵 · 78
3. 汉语颜色词的翻译 · 83

练习题 · 86

实践篇

翻译实训 · 89

1. 新时代的中国青年 · 89
2. 中国的粮食安全 · 97
3. 元宵节的起源 · 103
4. 作为中国文化"名片"的瓷器 · 107
5. 京剧脸谱的绚烂之美 · 110
6. 年画:渲染过年的热闹气氛 · 113

7. 刺绣:十指下的春风 ······ 118

8. 皮影戏:灯和影的艺术 ······ 122

9. 茶文化 ······ 128

10. 武术——拳术 ······ 132

11. 书法 ······ 137

12. 长城 ······ 142

参考文献 ······ 147

理论篇

THEORY

第一章 翻译概述

1. 翻译的性质

早在两千年前,人类就开始了翻译活动。作为人类最复杂的活动之一,翻译涉及人的认知、审美、性别、语言文化修养、外在社会环境、历史文化、语言特性等因素。数千年,人们对翻译的探究从未停止,不同学派从不同的角度对翻译活动展开了研究。语言学派运用现代语言学理论,深入翻译行为,研究翻译中语言的对等。英国著名翻译家卡特福德(Catford,1965)认为翻译是将一种语言(源语)的文本材料转换成另一种语言(目的语)的文本材料。(Translation may be defined as follows: the replacement of textual material in one language [SL] by equivalent textual material in another language[TL].) 尤金·奈达(Eugene A. Nida,1969),作为语言学派的代表人物之一,提出翻译是指在译语中用最贴近而又自然的对等语再现源语的信息,首先是语义,其次是风格。(Translating consists in reproducing in the receptor language the equivalent of the source language message, first in terms of meaning and secondly in terms of style.)彼得·纽马克(Peter Newmark,1988)指出翻译是将一种文本信息以原作者期望的方式用另一种语言表现出来。(Translation is rendering the meaning of a text into another language in the way that the author intended the text.)《牛津英语词典》中对"翻译"的定义是从一种语言转换成另一种语言。(Translation is to turn from one language into another.)《辞海》和《汉语大词典》给翻译的定义是把一种语言文字的意义用另一种语言文字表达出来。我国翻译家张培基(1983)提出,翻译是运用一种语言把另一种语言所表达的思想内容准确而完整地重新表达出来的语言活动。王宏印认为翻译是以译者为主体,以语言为转换媒介的创造性思维活动。所谓翻译,就是把见诸一种语言的文本用另一种语言准确而完整地再造出来,使译作获得与原作相当的文献价值或文学价值。冯庆华认为,翻译是许多语言活动中的一种,它是用一种语言形式把另一种语言形式里的内容重新表现出来的语言实践活动。

通过上述对翻译的定义可知,翻译是一个复杂的思维活动过程。译者需要关注源语文本信息、语言风格、作者写作意图、社会文化背景及自身主体性,将源语的文本信息、语言风格、读者效果、文本价值用另一种语言在新的文化背景下重新进行构建。

2. 翻译单位

翻译过程中语素、词、词组、小句、句子甚至段落和语篇均能充当翻译单位,因为它们在译文中均有某种形式的对应语言层次或单位,但从语素到句子的任一语言层次均不能独自作为翻译单位,机械地将某一语言层次作为翻译单位无法有效地完成翻译任务。

翻译单位是一个多元动态系统,在翻译过程中,翻译单位受翻译主体与翻译客体的影响而不断变化。选择翻译单位的过程即选择翻译方法的过程。

有学者认为翻译的基本单位是小句。持此观点的学者认为翻译转换操作主要在小句的层面进行。首先,以小句作为翻译的基本单位是因为译者认知加工的基本内容是命题,而小句是命题的具体语言表达形式。其次,小句的长度符合工作记忆容量限制的要求。最后,小句是话语中最灵活的语言成分,译者可以根据话语分析的需要在翻译中灵活地转换,实现原文与译文的对等。也有学者认为翻译的基本单位是句子,因为句子具有独立的信息结构和完整的句法形式,且能被短期记忆加工。还有学者指出翻译单位是段落,他们认为以段落作为翻译单位能帮助译者注意句与句之间的连接和逻辑关系,以及段落之间的衔接,段落与语篇的关系。只有考虑到了这些关系,译文才能保留原文的基本结构和意义。还有学者坚持翻译应以语篇作为基本翻译单位,因为译者不能因强调文本内容而牺牲整体结构,翻译应该是建立在文本整体意义上的语篇转换,寻求的是语篇意义的对应。

总的来看,所有层次的语言单位均有资格成为翻译单位,在翻译任务中各司其职。事实上,高级阶单位,比如段落、语篇可作为分析单位;低级阶单位,如语素、词、词组、小句、句子可作为转换单位。将翻译单位分为分析单位和转换单位的观点有助于弥合学者们对于翻译单位大小的分歧。译者对翻译转换单位的选择是一个动态过程,因为译者要综合考虑文本类型、翻译策略等因素而选用不同级阶的翻译转换单位。纽马克认为,权威型文本的翻译单位主要是词,信息型文本的翻译单位主要是固定搭配(collocation)和词组,召唤型文本的翻译单位主要是句子和语篇。王云桥认为,召唤型文本(如散文和小说)的翻译单位是段落。卡特福德和图里认为,采用意译翻译策略时,译者应以段落或语篇作为翻译单位;而采用直译翻译策略时,译者应以句子、短语、词或者语素作为翻译单位。

3. 翻译过程

西方翻译理论语言学派代表人物之一尤金·奈达(2001)针对翻译过程提出了分析、转换、重组和检验四个步骤。翻译是一个复杂的创作过程,第一步都需要从分析开始,随后经过转换及译入语表达,进入译文检测步骤。

原文分析需要译者分析单词与词组之间的语法关系,单词与词组承载的指称意义、内涵意义、情感意义、逻辑关系,原文的写作背景,作者的写作意图,篇章衔接等。转换阶段是翻译过程的核心,是介于分析和重组之间的一个步骤,是指译者把在大脑中分析好的语言材料从源语转换为译入语的过程,这一过程需要译者调整源语结构,对源语语段、句、词进行适地调整,脱离源语语言搭配,形成概念、感受或图像,最大限度地保留源语概念的准确性和完整性,以及译文行文的流畅性。在重构阶段,译者要将所有分析理解的内容,在尊重译入语文化、社会、读者认知背景、译入语语言特质的前提下,流畅地表达出来,并力争译文同原文产生相同的阅读效果与文本价值。在检测阶段,译者应检测译文的准确性、可读性,以及等效性。翻译过程中,译者的思维认知过程不是严格地按一个阶段紧跟另一个阶段进行的过程,而是一个综合过程,译者可从重组阶段向分析阶段推进,也可以在分析与转换步骤之间来回切换。优秀的译者还需要在分析阶段充分考虑转换和重构过程可能出现的情况。

(1) 分析

无论汉译英,还是英译汉,分析理解原文都是翻译过程的第一步。中西方思维模式的差异,影响到语言的基本结构、用词选句、词汇的文化内涵、联想内涵及情感内涵、篇章结构及衔接方式等。翻译过程中,译者分析汉语原文,对看似结构松散的句子进行结构划分,将隐藏于字里行间的隐性逻辑关系做显性化处理,从而输出形式衔接明显且逻辑关系严密的英文文本。分析英语原文时,往往需要充分调动语法知识,理清原文篇章衔接特性、句子成分、语义逻辑,以及文本所承载的文化、认知信息,必要时需要对长句进行切分,以充分理解原文信息与语言风格。

> 网络强国
> a country with strong cyber technology

汉语中,中心词为"国","强"作为形容词,是对"国"的修饰,而国家所强的方面是"网络",对原文理解后可以输出 a country with strong cyber technology、a country that excels in cyber technology 或 a country with cutting-edge cyber technology 等译文。

> 安得广厦千万间,大庇天下寒士俱欢颜!
> How I wish I could have ten thousand houses, to provide shelter for all who need it!
> (http://www.china.org.cn/chinese/2018—01/05/content_50195196.htm)

原文中的"寒士"原意有两种:一是出身低微的读书人,即 a poor scholar;二是贫困的人,即 poor people。此处意思显然更靠近第二种,但所指更广,应译为 all who need it,拓宽了涵盖范围。此外,文中的"广厦"也并不宜强调其"广",译为 house 即可。

> 他幼时家境贫穷,生活困难。
> Born into a poor family, he led a hard life in his early childhood.
> (庄绎传《英汉翻译简明教程》)

原文看似两句话并列无重心,但实则"生活困难"是重心,"幼时家境贫穷"是其条件,译作过去分词作状语。

> 他们正在为实现一个理想而努力,这个理想是每个中国人所珍爱的,在过去,许多中国人曾为了这个理想而牺牲了自己的生命。
> They are striving for the ideal which is close to the heart of every Chinese and for which, in the past, many Chinese have laid down their lives.

中文不怕重复,三次提到同一词汇"理想",其中后两个"理想"均指第一个"理想",是典型的形散意不散的表达。由于英文的形合表达需要,在翻译时需要以指代词或定语从句等实现显性衔接,译文中用了两个定语从句来避免重复,加强衔接。

(2) 转换

分析阶段之后,就到了由源语向译入语转换的阶段,这一关键步骤往往在译者的大脑中进行。转换过程中,译者不仅要关注各个核心句,还应该关注核心句之间的关系,使其按照一定关系有序输出。

奈达(2004)将核心句间的关系分为三大类型:时间关系、空间关系和逻辑关系。时间关系是指按照时间的先后顺序排列核心句。在原文中,如果句子并未按照时间次序排列,译者需要按照时间先后顺序将核心信息串联在一起。空间关系是指物体相互之间的关系和说话人与所指物体之间的关系。译者需要按照一定空间顺序,如从左到右、从上至下、由远及近等次序,有序地转换信息。逻辑关系是指核心句之间的因果关系、条件推断、目的方式等关系。译者需要打破原文的表层结构,按照实际逻辑关系梳理信息概念。

① **语义调整**

在转换的过程中,译者的首要任务就是确保语义的准确性与完整性,不能随意翻译或漏译。由于源语与目的语间巨大的语言文化差异,译者需要对源语语义进行适当的调整,具体方法有:习语翻译调整、比喻翻译调整、泛指语义或特指语义调整、简化冗余信息、语义重新分布及增补上下文等。

a. *习语翻译调整*

习语是最具文化特色、最能反映社会文化生活的语言表达,仅用简短的表达形式即可生动传达语言概念。习语具有民族性、地域性、阶级性、固定性、修辞性等特点,是人们对社会生活与人生哲理的总结与写照。习语特有的语言表达形式在日常使用中固定下来,具有一定的修辞效果及审美价值(Nida, 2004)。因此,翻译习语需要译者适当转换源语内容,具体方式有:变习语为非习语、借用译入语习语、变非习语为习语。

- 变习语为非习语

  塞翁失马,焉知非福。
  Misfortune may prove to be a blessing in disguise.
  此地无银三百两。
  A guilty person gives himself away by conspicuously protesting his innocence.
  失之东隅,收之桑榆。
  What one loses on the swings, one gets back on the roundabouts.

- 借用译入语习语

  物以类聚,人以群分。
  Birds of a feather flock together.
  无风不起浪。
  Where there's smoke, there's fire.
  天下没有不散的宴席。
  All good things must come to an end.

- 变非习语为习语

  谁都有糊涂的时候。
  Every man has a fool in his sleeve.
  天下没有谁都捞不着便宜的事。
  It is an ill wind that blows nobody good.
  两强相争,必有一斗。
  When Greek meets Greek, then comes the tug of war.

b. 比喻翻译调整

比喻凭借其植根于文化的联想意义使语言生动形象,具有极强的修辞效果。翻译中,源语与译入语间巨大的社会文化差异,使广大译者在翻译比喻时倍感压力与苦恼。如果按照原文的表达内容进行翻译,增加译文的修辞效果并被译文读者理解,固然为上上策,但是,语言文化差异使直译比喻在很多时候将译文变得晦涩难懂,不易被译入语读者接受。因此,当直译不能保留原文比喻的联想意义及形象性时，译者需要对源语内容进行适当调整，具体方法有：变比喻为非比喻、借用译入语中现有的比喻、在译入语中将原文中的非比喻语言改为比喻。

- **变比喻为非比喻**

他站在台上呆若木鸡。
He was frozen on the stage.

- **借用译入语中现有的比喻**

多如牛毛
as plentiful as black berries
骨瘦如柴
as thin as a shadow
他像狐狸一样狡猾。
He is as cunning as a dead pig.

- **在译入语中将原文中非比喻语言改为比喻**

他一夜鼾声不断。
He was dragging a pig to the market last night.
我感到浑身不自在。
I feel like a fish out of water.

c. 泛指语义或特指语义调整

这种调整方式是指改变原文的泛指语义用具体语义进行翻译，或改变原文的具体语义用泛指语义进行翻译。英语中缺乏表示"哥哥""弟弟""姐姐""妹妹""堂哥/姐""堂弟/妹""表哥/姐""表弟/妹"等的特指词汇，而多有泛指词汇，如"brother""sister""cousin"等。汉译英时需要调整词汇指称的范畴，以符合译入语的表达习惯。

d. 简化冗余信息

原文中，常常会因为语篇衔接方式、文本修辞、词汇搭配习惯或作者对信息进行强调等，而出现冗余信息。如果不对这些冗余信息进行调整，直接将其翻译出来，势必会大大影响译文的流畅度及可读性。

朵朵鲜花满园盛开。
Flowers bloom all over the yard.

今日各自进去,孤孤凄凄,举目无亲,须要自己保重!
Today, entering for the examination, you are going to be entirely on your own, so you'll have to take care of yourselves!

(曹雪芹《红楼梦》)

他决定洗心革面,重新做人。
He was determined to turn over a new leaf.

(冯庆华《实用翻译教程》)

e. 语义重新分布

翻译时不太可能出现字字对应的情况,译者通常会将原文中的一个词翻译成译文中的一个词组,甚至一句话;同样,译者也可能将原文中的一个词组或一个小句译为一个词。

他本不该占她的便宜。
He shouldn't have taken advantage of her financially.

你必须在九点之前回来。没有商量的余地。
You must come back home before 9 o'clock. Period.

f. 增补上下文

译者需要面对的不仅仅是两种不同的语言符号,更是两种不同的社会与文化。为了既保留源语的形象表达,不引起歧义,又满足译入语读者的阅读需求,译者需要在译文中增补内容。

不要重复叶公好龙那个故事。
The story of Lord Ye who professed to love dragons should not be repeated.

班门弄斧
Show off one's proficiency with axe before Lu Ban, the master carpenter.

②**结构调整**

在合理转换语义信息的基础上，译者应调整原文语言结构，以确保译入语表达的流畅性。结构调整主要涉及以下几方面：话语结构、句子结构、单词结构、语音结构。（Nida，2004）

a. 话语结构

调整话语结构主要涉及直接引语与间接引语间的转换、篇章衔接方式的转换、人称转换及时态转换等。

b. 句子结构

句子常常被视作翻译单位，因此句子层面的转换最为常见。句子结构调整主要涉及以下几方面：语序、双重否定、单复数的一致、主动结构与被动结构、并列结构与偏正结构、同位结构、省略、内隐关系的说明。

· 语序

语序能够体现一个民族的语言习惯及逻辑思维方式，也是句子表意的关键。汉英两种语言的巨大差异要求译者在翻译过程中对语序进行较大调整。

> 她一字不漏地记下所说的话。
> She took down what was said, careful not to miss a word.
> 他目睹了战后波及各领域的经济危机。
> He witnesses the post-war economic crisis that prevailed in various fields.

· 双重否定

双重否定在一些文本中相当于肯定，在另一些文本中却是否定的强调式。在准确理解的基础上，译者需要对原文的双重否定进行适当调整，再现原文中双重否定的语义概念及修辞效果。

> 他们没有一天不吵架。
> A whole day had never passed without their quarrel.
> 没有孩子不爱吃糖。
> All kids love candies.

· 单复数的一致

英语要求谓语动词与主语保持数的一致，而汉语却没有此类要求。因此，中文英译时,译者需要对原文的主谓搭配进行适当调整,以符合译入语的表达习惯。

> 在老师的帮助下,他取得了巨大进步。
> He has made great progress with the help of teachers.
> 谋事在人,成事在天。
> Man proposes, God disposes.

• 主动结构与被动结构

英语是形合语言,注重语言结构的显性表达,其语态、时态及语气均为显性;汉语是意合语言,动词没有屈折形态变化,而且表示被动的词汇在一些表达中也被直接省去,只剩下被动语义。因此,中文英译时,译者需要根据译入语的表达习惯,作适当增减。

此外,被动使用的频次及场合在汉英两种语言中也存在巨大差异。英语中被动语态的使用有助于强化叙事的客观性,而汉语中被动语态的使用则多有消极情态色彩。基于汉英两种语言在被动语态上的巨大差异,译者需要对原文本中被动语态进行适当调整。

> 我方顾客急需以上货品。
> All the terms mentioned above are urgently required by our customers.
> 这类广告随处可见。
> This sort of advertisement can be seen everywhere.

• 并列结构与偏正结构

调整句子中的并列结构和偏正结构也是译者应当注意的方面。

> 很暖和
> nice and warm
> 不停地发抖
> shook and tremble
> 着实吃了一惊
> was surprised and taken back
> 他的确死了。
> He is dead and gone.

· 同位结构

在一些文本中,同位结构并不十分明显,如果译者不作适当调整,译文将出现明显错误。

> 北京这座城市
> the city of Beijing

· 省略

虽然汉英两种语言都使用省略构建句子,但省略的形式及频次都大不相同。汉语是意合语言,语言结构多隐性,陈述句也常常会省略句子的主语。而英语是形合语言,陈述句中的主语通常不会省略。因此,译者在处理省略成分时,需进行适当调整,不能按照原文的语言结构进行翻译。

> 看着这些老照片,心里掠过一丝歉意。
> Looking at these old photos, I couldn't help feeling rather regretful.
> 沉默啊,沉默啊!不在沉默中爆发,就在沉默中灭亡。
>
> (鲁迅《纪念刘和珍君》)
>
> Silence, silence! Unless we burst out, we shall perish in this silence!
>
> (杨宪益 戴乃迭 译)

· 内隐关系的说明

汉英两种语言都包含不言而喻的内隐信息,但这种信息只局限于特定范围,翻译时需要调整表达形式具体说明,以避免译文意义含糊和产生歧义。

> 他是他唯一的朋友。
> Mike was his only friend.
> 我在他父亲身上找不到一点学者气质。
> I can't find any scholarship in his father.

c. 单词结构

翻译中,译者需要对原文词性、词汇的形态、敬语的使用等方面做适当调整,以达到交际目的。

战争不断消耗着国内资源。

The war is a drain on national resources.

为此,我非常赞成修复长城,非常赞成给赞助修复长城的人刻碑留名。

(张辛欣 桑晔《北京人——奉献》)

I'm all for repairing the Great Wall and inscribing the contributor's names.

d. 语音结构

翻译外来词汇时,音译是常见方式之一,译者可采用以下几种方式。

一是完全改变原文的语音结构,以符合译语的读音规则。如把 Peter 译成"彼得";把 Paris 译成"巴黎"。二是照搬外来的形式,不考虑外来词是否合乎译语的读音规则。如把"北京"译成"Beijing";把 Chomsky 仍写作 Chomsky。三是折中法。对于人们熟悉的专有名词,如果译语中没有文字传统,译者需照搬原文语音结构;如果译语有文字传统,翻译时便遵循译语的语音结构。对于人们不熟悉的专有名词,译者按译语的语音规则进行翻译。

(3)表达

奈达(2004)认为译入语语内重组就是对转换过的文本进行词汇、句法、语篇特征等层面的组织,以便读者最大限度地理解欣赏译文。实践证明,在完成对原文的分析和语际转换之后,译文质量完全取决于译入语语内重构的成败。语际转换的过程只是将原文的基本含义传达到译入语中,语际转换过后的文本只能算是译文的概念基础,最终译文的确定还需要词汇、句法、语篇层面的重组和整合。在奈达看来,译入语语内重组是在文体的框架内进行的。在《翻译理论与实践》一书中,奈达专章论述了译入语重组,指出在完成源语到译入语的信息转换之后的译入语语内重组的过程中,译者应着重考虑以下三点:理想的语言变体或文体变体、各种不同文体的要素和特征、表达理想文体所使用的翻译技巧。

(4)检验

尽管检验译文与分析、转换和重组这三个过程有所不同,但就迅速暴露译文中存在的问题而言,这是一个十分重要的环节。过去,译文的检验大都是指定一名懂得源语和译语的人来进行原文和译文的比较,测定译文与原文的对应程度。这个方法的缺点是,这位懂得双语的鉴定人可能已经熟悉文本和内容的类型,用不着花太多精力就能理解译文。因此,对译文进行正确的评估,只能是通过对只懂译语的读者进行检测得出的结论来实现。

可选择的有效的检测方法有以下四种:邀请几位读者朗读译文;仔细分析朗读者的面部表情;请听过译文朗读的人向没有听过朗读的人讲述内容;填空检测法。

最有效的检测方式之一是请几位水平高的人来朗读译文,译者一边看着稿子,一边标记朗读时打磕巴、误读、用错词替换、重复,以及语调把握不定的地方。如果两个或几个译入语水平相当的人都在同一地方产生疑惑,这些地方就明显有问题。造成朗读不畅的问题有以下几种:高层次的词汇;句法蹩脚;缺乏过渡词;并列的词汇中辅音群发音浊重;没有表示疑问、命令、讽刺、反语和省略的标记词。这种检测方法并不能告诉译者应该怎么去修改译文,但能够指出译文中需要修改的地方。

当不同的人朗读译文时,译者要仔细观察他们的面部表情,特别是他们的眼神。因为表情和眼神可以反映出他们对译文内容和形式的理解和领会的程度。细心而又善解人意的观察者很快就能发现:朗读者是读懂了译文,还是对它的内容不知所云;是对译文的内容感兴趣,还是觉得枯燥无味;读来饶有兴致,还是觉得译文太难而无法诵读。

对译文内容的检验,最好是请一个人朗读或默读译文,然后让他向其他人讲述内容。令人吃惊的是,许多人读完了却不知所云,但如果有两个或几个人在理解上犯了相同的错误,那么显然就需要修改译文。当然,如果原文本身有意要含混模糊,则可另当别论。

填空检测法也是测定译文可读性的有效方法。这个方法是每四个词后面空一处,再请人根据上下文要求填入恰当的词。在至少五十个空里能够填对多少词语有效地显示了转换概率的范围,从而也就测定了译文的可读性和可理解的程度。这个方法也可以变通一下,即每九个词后面空一处,再请人朗读译文,然后计算朗读者填错的地方,并提出修改意见。

4. 译者的素养

译者是在两种语言之间进行文字、文化和思想沟通的桥梁,因此,并不是学过外语的人都可以做翻译。翻译的特点对译者的素质提出了更高的要求。就中文英译而言,译者应该具有以下素质。

首先,要有严肃负责的工作态度。译者必须对原作负责,对读者负责,反复修改译稿,以达到最佳传播效果。

其次,要有较高的汉语水平和英语水平。作为以汉语为母语的译者,往往会忽略不断提高自身汉语水平的要求。在英译汉中,汉语水平的高低直接关系译文是否能准确传达原文信息,是否清晰畅达,是否符合原文的风格特征,是否能吸引译文读者等,所以汉语的修养不可轻视。同时,译者也要有较高的英语水平,英语毕竟不是母语,学习英语更应精益求精,不仅要能够正确理解英语词汇和句子的含义,学会英语的各种表达方法,还要熟悉不同文体的行文风格,不断锤炼英语的表达能力。

再次,译者要掌握一定的专业知识和丰富的文化知识。俗话说"隔行如隔山",特别是专业性很强的科技文体、法律文件、经济合同等,不了解所译文章涉及的专业,就搞不清原文的全部意义,也就根本谈不上翻译。如果经常涉及某个专业领域的翻译,译者最好能够学习一些该专业的基础知识。除此之外,合格的译者还应该多了解本国和英语国家的历史、地理、风土人情、文化传统。只有这样,才能达到文化沟通的目的,不至于在一些文化内容的翻译上出差错。

最后,译者应该具备坚实的翻译理论基础,以理论指导实践,多学一些翻译名家的范文,经常进行翻译实践,这对不断提高翻译水平是很有帮助的。

练习题

一、思考题

1. 什么是翻译?
2. 什么是翻译单位?
3. 翻译过程中转换有几种类型?
4. 译者应具备哪些素养?

二、翻译以下句子,并解释在翻译过程中进行了哪些转换。

1. 好事多磨。
2. 天下无难事,只怕有心人。
3. 狗咬吕洞宾,不识好人心。
4. 情人眼里出西施。
5. 半瓶醋,出事故。
6. 别人家鸡零狗碎的事情你都知道的这么全。
7. 一直站在一旁观看的人开始鼓掌。
8. 这些客人受宠若惊。

9. 中华人民共和国已宣告成立。
10. 这样做无异于杀鸡取卵。
11. 一个巴掌拍不响。
12. 心脏检查应该被列为常规检查。
13. 我们终于摆脱了贫困。
14. 没人不知道他酷爱流行乐。
15. 最后两个字特别用力。

第二章 英汉语言对比

1. 英汉语义对比

英汉语义可以从词、短语、句子三个层次进行对比。

（1）词

表示实体的词，在英汉两种语言中实现语义对等并不难。例如 bird（鸟）、lion（狮子）、book（书）、person（人），这些词在英汉两种语言中的含义均很明确，也无明显文化差异，翻译时比较容易。

具有抽象意义的词，尽管其核心语义并无较大差异，但因其各自蕴含的文化元素不同，其语义在两种语言中存在差异的可能较大。例如，将宣传译成 propagate，会让语义发生改变。汉语中的"宣传"是中性词，而英文中的 propagate 表示传播带有偏见的消息，因此在翻译"宣传党的主张"时应避开 propagate 这样带有负面色彩的词，而使用"communicating the Party's propositions"。

（2）短语

翻译英汉短语或词组搭配时，需将其看成一个整体理解，因为如果将其切分为一个个独立的词，然后连接起来，可能会造成语义对等错误。例如，看到 white elephant 如果望文生义，便会理解为"白色大象"，但它真正的意思是"昂贵而无用之物"。yellow dog 中，因"yellow"在英文中含有"妒忌；懦弱"等意，因此译为"忘恩负义之徒"；而 lucky dog 则与中文中的"幸运儿"在语义上对等。类似的例子有 go viral（疯传）、at first blush（乍一看）、cash in（利用）等。

汉译英时，短语或词组搭配也因存在中英思维、文化差异而需对语义进行适当转换。例如"人类命运共同体"，在英文中如果继续沿用汉语中名词的顺序，以名词堆积合成，译文中就无法体现名词间的逻辑关系。"命运"在英文词典中语义对等的词有"destiny"或"fate"，但"人类命运共同体"这个具有中国智慧的理念体现的是寻求人类共同利益和共同价值的内涵，用 destiny 或 fate 再现"命运"这个政治概念显然与原文不对等,因此译为 shared future。"人类命运共同体"译为"A Community of Shared Future for Mankind"。

(3) 句子

英汉句子层面的语义对比仍以词汇、短语层面的对比为基础。例如:

It's time to turn plough into sword.

该努力的时候到了。

该句中的 plough 语义为犁,sword 语义为剑,表层含义为"该是把犁变成剑的时候了",但要让译文在译语读者中产生对等反应,需将其深层语义译出,即为"该努力的时候到了"。

The dust hasn't settled yet.

调查仍在进行之中。

the dust has settled 在英文中表示"烟消云散",the dust hasn't settled 的表层语义则表示"尘埃仍未落定",可根据语境引申为"事件仍在处理之中"或"调查仍在进行之中"等。

He finally issued a full-throated apology.

他最终郑重道歉了。

full-throated 表层语义为"声音洪亮的",但在本句中直译为表层语义显然不准确,需引申为"郑重的"等。

倡导简约适度、绿色低碳的生活方式,反对奢侈浪费和不合理消费,开展创建节约型机关、绿色家庭、绿色学校、绿色社区和绿色出行等行动。

We encourage simple, moderate, green, and low-carbon ways of life, and oppose extravagance and excessive consumption. We will launch initiatives to make Party and government offices do better when it comes to conservation, and develop eco-friendly families, schools, communities, and transport services.

(language. chinadaily. com. cn/19thcpcnationalcongress/2107—11/06/content_34188086_5. htm)

原文中多次出现"绿色",英文中与之对应的词为 green,但"绿色学校"等中的"绿色"如果译为 green,则与原文的语义不同,因此应处理为 eco-friendly。

2. 句法结构对比

英汉两种语言在句序上有一定的差异,如英语简单句的句序一般是"主语＋谓语＋宾语＋状语",而汉语单句一般是"主语＋状语＋谓语＋宾语",例如:I had breakfast at home.(我在家吃了早饭。)英语的状语从句、定语从句的位置与汉语的也不尽相同。整体来说,英汉在句法结构上存在的异同可以归为以下几类:主语与主题、形合与意合、树状与竹状、静态与动态。

（1）主语与主题

英语属于主语显著语言,汉语属于主题显著语言。西方人提倡以概念为基础的判断和推理,反映在句子上,就是主谓结构框架,即由主语占据第一个语法位置,谓语占据第二个语法位置。相比之下,汉语句子的施事主体通常蕴含在行为事件的主观表现中,即主体与客体可以合而为一,因此汉语句子可以无主语,以主题形式表达内容,常出现"主题—评论"式句子结构。

> I did not remember a single point discussed at the meeting.
> 会上讲了什么,我一点儿没记住。
> I was sad to hear what happened to you and your family last week.
> 听到上周你和你的家人所经历的一切,我很难过。

英文原文中均有主语,但汉语译文并未按原文的主谓语序进行表达,而是调整为"主题—评论"式的表达。

> 改革开放以来,中国发生了巨大的变化。
> Great changes have taken place in China since the introduction of the reform and opening policy.
> 生活在奴才们中间,做奴才们的首领,我将引为生平的最大耻辱、最大的悲哀。
> I would regard it as the deepest disgrace and sorrow of my life to live among the flunkeys and become their chief.
>
> （张培基《英译中国现代散文选（一）》）

中文原文主语不显著,但主题明确,英文按照主谓结构进行再现,主语可以是人称,也可以是物称。

(2) 形合与意合

汉语意合重于形合,英语形合重于意合。"形合"(hypotaxis))指借助语言形式手段(包括词汇手段和形态手段)显示句法关系,实现词语或句子的连接;"意合"(parataxis)指不借助语言形式手段而借助词语或句子的意义或逻辑联系实现它们之间的连接。前者注重语句形式上的接应(cohesion),后者注重行文意义上的连贯(coherence)。除词语级外,无论在句子级或语段级,英语的形式接应手段都比汉语多。(刘宓庆,2006)

> 一粥一饭,当思来之不易;
> 半丝半缕,恒念物力维艰。
> Remember that every bowl of rice and porridge has not been got easily.
> Be ever mindful that each cotton or sick garment has taken much material and labor to make.
>
> (陈宏薇《新实用汉译英教程》)

译文中"that""and""or"与"to"在原文中无对应表达,在译文中起到衔接作用。

(3) 静态与动态

英语的动词受形态规范和句法规范的约束,有定式和非定式之分,并各有其严谨的功能限制。英语以名词(和介词)占优势,静态中有动态,比较重理念。汉语重动态描写,就功能而言,以动词占优势,这是汉语重要的表现法之一。(刘宓庆,2010)英语每个句子中只能使用一个限定式动词(finite verb),唯一例外形式是并列句动词,而汉语中却存在着连动式。因此,英译汉时常要变静为动,摆脱名词化的框架和大量介词的干扰,突出汉语的动态色彩。

> I took it for granted that mothers were the sandwich-makers, the finger-painting appreciators and the homework monitors.
> 我觉得做母亲的给她的孩子制作三明治,鉴赏指画,检查他们的家庭作业,都是理所当然的事。
>
> (杨平《名作精译》)

We don't understand that pain may be telling us that we are eating too much or the wrong things, or that we are smoking too much or drinking too much, or that there is too much emotional congestion in our lives or that we are being worn down by having to cope daily with overcrowded streets and highways, the pounding noise of garbage grinders, or the cosmic distance between the entrance to the airport and the departure gate.

我们不明白,疼痛可能是在告诫我们,或吃得太饱,或吃得不当,或吸烟太多,或饮酒过度,或生活中煎熬太苦,或因每天都得面对拥挤的大街和公路、忍受垃圾粉碎机的撞击声和奔波于从机场入口到登机口之间的长距离而被搞得过分疲劳。

(乔萍 瞿淑蓉 宋洪玮《散文佳作108篇》)

原文中的非谓语动词、名词等以动词形式出现在汉语中,符合汉语行文习惯。在汉译英时常要变"动"为"静",突出译入语的静态色彩。

熟练的剪纸艺人剪纸的过程如同变魔术,他将一张红纸在手上左叠右叠,然后用剪刀轻轻地剪几下,摊开一看,就是一幅漂亮的图画。

A skilled paper-cutting craftsperson cuts paper into designs like doing magic tricks. A piece of red paper is folded and then cut several times, before being unfolded into an attractive picture.

(章思英 陈海燕 Insights into Chinese Culture)

剃下来的胎发不能随便扔掉,而是要放在一起,用丝线缠好,由母亲挂在孩子床头,据说可以保佑孩子平安成长。

The shaved fetal hair cannot be randomly thrown away but should be put together and bound by silk threads. Then the mother should hang it above the baby's bed, which is allegedly able to bless the baby to grow up safely.

(刘谦功 舒燕 于洁《中国文化欣赏读本上》)

哼,美国的橘子包着纸,遇到北平的带着霜儿的玉李,还不愧杀!

Indeed, America's paper-wrapped oranges will pale beside Peiping's plums bearing a thin coating of frostlike bloom!

(张培基《英译中国现代散文选(一)》)

> 而且真想做王的人,他将用他的手法去打天下,决不会放在口里说的。
> Moreover, if one is really bent on being a king, he will try to carry out his design by deeds instead of by words.
>
> (张培基《英译中国现代散文选(一)》)

原文中的动词在译文中或以名词形式再现意义,或以非谓语动词、介词加名词形式再现,确保了译文的地道性和可读性。

练习题

一、翻译下列内容,注意汉英差异。

1. 对中国人来说,红色是一种吉祥的颜色,代表了好运、名誉和财富。

2. 月饼是一种圆饼,里面有各种馅,表面装饰着各种有关节日传说的艺术图案。

3. 中国古代建筑十分注重整体布局和左右对称,象征了秩序和稳定。

4. 四合院和胡同是北京的两大特色,早已成为北京的象征。

5. 中国人民在古时就已经开始种植桑树,并将桑蚕驯化,开始饲养桑蚕和制造出质量上乘的蚕丝织品了。

6. 到了汉朝和唐朝,青铜在铜镜制造方面又重新显现了它的重要性,铜镜不仅是流行的和实用的物品,而且还是不可或缺的随葬物品。

7. 古人讲,"夫孝,德之本也"。自古以来,中国人就提倡尊老爱幼,倡导老吾老以及人之老、幼吾幼以及人之幼。

8. 汉语中的"年糕",和"年高"发音相同,因此象征着时运年和不断高升。

9. 风景如画的苏州园林,在有限空间里表现出微观世界,将山水、花草树木、亭台楼阁融为一体。

10.《诗经》全面展示了中国周朝时期的社会生活,真实地反映了中国奴隶社会从兴盛到衰败时期的历史面貌。

第三章 翻译与文化

文化涵盖了人类社会中的种种现象,包括艺术、音乐、舞蹈、仪式、宗教等表现形式,以及工具使用、烹饪和制衣等技术。物质文化的概念涵盖了文化的物理表达,例如技术、建筑和艺术,而非物质文化方面则包括社会组织原则、神话、哲学、文学、科学等。英国19世纪人类学家泰勒(1871)指出"文化或文明是作为一个社会成员所获得的知识、信仰、艺术、法律、道德、习俗及其他能力与习惯的综合体。"《辞海》将文化定义为"一定的人的群体创造和积累的物质财富和精神财富的总和。"由此可见文化不是单一的,而是多元化的,是人类在长期的发展过程中积累的所有成果。英国诗人马修·阿诺德曾说"文化是人对甜美和光明的憧憬,重要的是,要使这种憧憬超越一切"(刘宓庆,2016)。

翻译是语言的转换,而语言是文化的载体,因此翻译与文化密切相关。译者在进行汉英翻译时,一定要意识到文化在语言转换过程中的重要作用。茅盾曾经说过:"好的翻译,自然不是单纯技术性的语言外形的变易,而是要求译者通过原作的语言外形,深刻体会原作者的艺术创作过程,把握住原作的精神,在自己的思想、感情、生活体验中找到最适合的印证,然后运用适合于原作风格的文学语言,把原作的内容与形式正确无遗地再现出来(许钧,2012)。"由此可见,翻译的过程中,译者需要考虑源语体现的文化内涵,以此来采用适当的翻译策略将其再现。

1. 文化趋同与语言的融合

文化趋同指的是两种文化不断相互影响而变得越来越相似。基本上,文化之间的相互作用越多,它们的价值观、意识形态、行为、艺术和习俗就将开始相互反映。在通过通讯和运输技术及组织协会相互参与的文化之间,这种趋势尤其明显。

如今中西方的文化融合相较于中国改革开放初期有了较为明显的增强。结婚典礼上新娘穿西式白色婚纱,新郎穿西装已司空见惯,快餐文化深入社会的各个阶层,汉堡、三明治、比萨、牛排等西餐已经走入了千家万户,薯片、爆米花、咖啡、可乐成为人们闲暇时的休闲小食与饮品。西方的健身文化也进入了大众视野,越来越多的人加入了健身行列,举杠铃、健美操逐渐盛行。美剧、英剧、好莱坞电影、迪士尼动画等文娱产品,影响了越来越多的年轻人。节奏蓝调和说唱音乐等娱乐文化也让越来越多的年轻人着迷。

同时,中国的文化也在不断地影响着西方社会。中国的武术、京剧、传统工艺、服饰、饮食、教育、中医文化等受到了外国友人的欢迎。截至2021年底,全球共有180多个国家和地区开展了中文教育,76个国家将中文纳入国民教育体系,外国正在学习中文的人数超过2500万,累计学习和使用中文的人数接近2亿。足以见得中国文化的影响力。越来越多的外国友人申请到中国留学,学习中国文化,例如国家汉办主办的中文比赛节目《汉语桥》,就吸引了诸多外国朋友来参赛。西方有越来越多的城市在春节期间举行具有中国特色的庆祝活动,武术表演、书法、舞龙舞狮被更多的外国友人所了解,其中不乏很多外国朋友为了学习武术和书法而来到中国。现在,研究汉学的西方学者也日益增多,儒学、道家的哲学思想在西方也深受喜爱。中国的服饰文化在国际时装秀上大放异彩,汉唐风格的服饰在西方受到更多人的青睐。中餐馆在西方国家越开越多,让越来越多的外国朋友爱上了中国菜。

语言在文化交融的过程中起到了不可取代的媒介作用。通过语言,异国文化得以传播,异国的词汇、术语也通过语言得以在本土语言中使用。

早期中国的语言便经由文化进入英语语言。中国文化与西方文化交融的时候,诸多具有中国文化特色的词汇进入了西方文化当中。从17世纪开始,一些表达中国特有事物的汉语词汇就通过音译或者借译的手段进入英语,比如 jiaozi(饺子)、Mahjong(麻将)、yuan(元)、jiao(角)、fen(分)、yin yang(阴阳)、fengshui(风水)、Yamen(衙门)等。大多数汉语外来词都能做到与英语音似,少数会有一些差异,有一些汉语外来词在进入英语的过程中形式发生了一些变化。如:kowtow(叩头)、wonton(馄饨)、oolong(乌龙茶)、kongfu(功夫)、tofu(豆腐)、cheong-sam(旗袍)、ginseng(人参)、chow-mein(炒面)、dim-sum(点心)、litche(荔枝)。近些年,随着科技发展,汉语词汇在英语语言中的融合也逐步变多,例如在美国的在线词典 *Urban Dictionary* 中就收录了很多具有中国特色的词语,例如Tuhao(土豪)、gelivable(给力)等。《牛津英语词典》近些年也收录了诸多中国新词,例如 add oil(加油)、hongbao(红包)、guanxi(关系)、wuxia(武侠)、hukou(户口)、lose face(丢脸)、goji berry(枸杞)等。

在全球化的大背景下,中国与西方国家的交流和沟通变得越来越频繁。中国的文化与西方的文化也在潜移默化中进行了融合。随着西方文化进入中国,许多带有西方文化特色的词语也渐渐成为人们的日常用词,如汉堡包(hamburger)、巴士(bus)、咖啡(coffee)、酒吧(bar)、扑克(poker)、吉他(guitar)、沙发(sofa)、拷贝(copy)、摩托(motor)、芒果(mango)、尼龙(nylon)、丁克(dink)等。这些词汇在汉语中的出现,反映了不同时期文化融合的特色,也例证了中西方文化的融合趋势。

互联网的发展促成了"地球村"的形成,全球的文化、政治、经济等领域有着不同程度的沟通与交流。不同国家的人们通过媒体、网络等途径了解到了其他国家的文化,在这个过程当中也在潜移默化中影响了语言的表达。在日常生活中,人们会将汉语与英语进行融合表达,如"加入WTO""GDP增长""VIP特权""做CT""验DNA""发现UFO""GPS导航"等。"Hi""Hello""Fine""What""Anyway""OK""Bye-bye""Yes""No"等简单的英语已经融入了人们的日常交流用语。诸如此类的例子不胜枚举,足以见得文化的趋同导致语言的变化。

2. 文化差异与翻译

文化是不同民族在长期的历史发展过程中累积下来的物质和精神财富的总和,每一个民族都有与其相适应的文化。各民族不同的文化决定了其不同的建筑、服饰、饮食、价值观、思维方式、审美情趣、宗教信仰等。由此可见,文化既有表层的物质文化,也有深层的精神文化。语言与文化紧密相连,语言是在特定社会文化中产生的特定产物,同时,语言又是文化的载体和文化传播的媒介。因此,不同的文化造就了不同的语言。

翻译作为语际交际,不仅涉及语言的转换,也包括文化的移植。吕叔湘曾经说过"翻译家必须是一个杂家"(罗新璋,2009),所谓的"杂",就是要求译者要具备广博的知识。任何的翻译都不能脱离文化,简单的语言转换并不能跨越文化差异的鸿沟。文化与语言既相互影响又相互制约。翻译家尤金·奈达(2001)曾说过,"由于词语的意思是体现在特定的文化背景当中,因此只有充分了解两种文化才能得出成功的译文。"

(1) 生态文化差异与翻译

生态指的是植物、动物、人类相互作用的方式。不同的国家在地理、环境、自然等方面存在着诸多的差异,由此导致生态文化的差异,并最终形成了与生态文化相关的语言上的差异。由于文化差异,很多词汇在不同的文化当中具有不同的联想意义。在中国文化当中,就有许多具有中国特色的生态文化负载词,如梅、兰、竹、菊。梅、兰、竹、菊在西方文化中没有特别的文化内涵,而在我国文化中却是感物喻志的象征,用来代表君子。此外,由于中西方生态文化存在差异,很多文化负载词在西方语言中并没有对等的词汇。此类词汇在翻译的时候可以采用释义或加注释等方式。

> 夏练三伏,冬练三九。
>
> 这一谚语,描述勤奋努力的人在一年中最冷最热的时候仍然在锻炼。其中的"三伏"和"三九"是非常具有中国生态文化特色的词汇,在英语中没有与其对应的词汇。"三九"指的是冬至节后第十九天至第二十七天,通常是一年中最冷的时期。"三伏"指的是夏至节后的头伏、二伏、三伏,通常是一年中最热的时期。因此,"三伏"和"三九"可以采用释义的方法将其分别翻译成"the hottest days in summer"和"the coldest days in winter"。

> 正月十四的夜,是我不肯轻易便睡,等候他们的仪仗从床下出来的夜,然而仍然只是看见几个光着身子的隐鼠在地面游行,不像正在办着喜事。
>
> (鲁迅《朝花夕拾》)
>
> On the eve of Lantern Festival, I was always reluctant to go to sleep as I waited for that procession to emerge from under my bed. But all I saw were the same few mice wearing no clothes and parading the floor as usual but attending my wedding apparently.
>
> (杨宪益 戴乃迭 译)

"正月十四的夜"是中国的农历正月十五元宵节的前一天的晚上,如果按照西方的阳历来翻译的话,没有具体对应的日期,因此,此处将其意译成了"On the eve of Lantern Festival",来弥补西方文化中该生态文化词汇的缺失,使读者明了"正月十四"不是普通的日子,而是中国重要节日的前一天。

(2) 物质文化差异与翻译

物质文化是指人类创造的物质产品体现出的文化,包括所用的工具、技术和艺术,体现了人的生存方式、生存状态和思想感情。由于处于不同社会的人们在长期的劳动生活中形成了不同的物质过程和物质产品,有些只存在于特定的社会中,即便是一样的东西,在不同的文化中其联想意义也不一样。例如旗袍、乌纱帽、麻将、象棋、轿子、炕等在西方社会并不存在。

> 陋室空堂,当年笏满床。
>
> 　　　　　　　　　　　　　　　　　　　　　　　　　(《红楼梦》)
>
> Mean huts and empty halls.
> Where emblems of nobility once hung.
>
> 　　　　　　　　　　　　　　　　　　　　　　　　　(杨宪益　戴乃迭 译)

"笏"是古代大臣上朝拿着的手板,用玉、象牙或竹片制成。"满床笏"是一个典故,说的是唐朝名将汾阳王郭子仪六十大寿时,七子八婿皆来祝寿,由于他们都是朝廷里的高官,手中皆有笏板,拜寿时把笏板放满床头,所以"满床笏"这一典故后来就被用来借喻家门福禄昌盛、富贵寿考。在此处这两句出自《红楼梦》,在这里"笏满床"形容家里做大官的人多。"笏"是身份地位的象征,是高贵的象征,因此译为"emblems of nobility"。

> 将道人肩上褡裢抢了过来背着……
>
> 　　　　　　　　　　　　　　　　　　　　　　　　　(《红楼梦》)
>
> He transferred the sack from the Taoist's shoulder to his own…
>
> 　　　　　　　　　　　　　　　　　　　　　　　　　(杨宪益　戴乃迭 译)

"褡裢"是一种中间开口而两端装东西的口袋,大的可以搭在肩上,小的可以挂在腰带上。由于在西方文化中没有"褡裢",因此在翻译的时候需要将其实际所指译出来。由于"褡裢"的材质一般是麻布的,因此此处翻译成了"sack"。

> 取一张桌子,供奉香炉、烛台、魂幡,俱各停当。
>
> 　　　　　　　　　　　　　　　　　　　　　　　　　(《儒林外史》)
>
> He also set a table there with incense-burners, candle sticks and pennons to call back the spirit.
>
> 　　　　　　　　　　　　　　　　　　　　　　　　　(杨宪益　戴乃迭 译)

"魂幡"是一种垂直悬挂的旗子,丧葬时用以招引鬼魂。同样,它在西方文化中不存在,因此译文中对其进行了释译,即用来召唤魂魄的旗子。

> 家景正在坏下去,常听到父母愁<u>柴米</u>。
>
> (鲁迅《朝花夕拾》)
>
> I often heard my parents worrying as to <u>where our next meal was to come from</u>.
>
> (杨宪益　戴乃迭译)

"柴米"意思是柴和米,泛指日常最必需的生活资料,在此处指的是一日三餐,"愁柴米"也就是发愁下一顿饭从哪里来。如果直接译为"柴"和"米",目的语读者可能不理解其真正含义,因此译者在此没有直译,而是通过意译的方式将"柴米"译为"next meal",也就是其实际意义,这样有利于目的语读者理解原文。

汉语中有许多物质文化词汇在西方国家不存在,如下例:

牌匾 inscription

戒尺 ferule

轿子 sedan-chair

高跷 silt-walkers

算盘 abacus

四合院 Siheyuan (a courtyard surrounded by buildings on all four sides)

象棋 Chinese chess

盘缠 money

(3) 社会文化差异与翻译

社会文化包括社会风俗和习惯、信仰和价值观念、行为规范、生活方式、文化传统等诸多方面。中西方的社会文化在很多方面都存在着较大的差异性。中国崇尚集体主义,而西方倾向于个人主义。中国文化中的传统节日在西方社会并不存在,因此,庆祝不同节日的习俗对于外国友人来说也是非常陌生。汉语中对人的称谓较之于西方也是非常复杂,例如,连襟、妯娌、太婆婆、重孙子、孙媳妇、姑姥姥、姑姥爷、姨姥姥、姨姥爷、大姑姐、表哥、堂哥等。英语中的称谓就相对来讲简单很多,sister in law、brother in law、cousin、aunt、uncle 等比较单一的称谓,并不能明确表示人与人之间具体的亲属关系。同时,中西方文化中关于社会风俗习惯与社会礼节的差异也较大。

> 新的是写情书,少则一束,多则一捆;旧的是什么"问名","采纳",磕头作揖。
>
> （鲁迅《朝花夕拾》）
>
> The new way is to write love letters, at least one packet if not a whole sheaf; the old way was to "inquire names," "send betrothal gifts," kowtow and bow.
>
> （杨宪益　戴乃迭 译）

"问名"和"采纳"是中国旧时婚姻礼仪"六礼"中的两个,其中"问名"指的是男家具书托媒请问女子的名字和生辰,"采纳"即纳采,旧时男方欲与女方结亲,男方家需遣媒妁往女方家提亲,送礼求婚。由于中西方的婚俗有差异,因此,译者在翻译时没有音译,而是进行了释译,将其分别处理成"inquire names"和"send betrothal gifts",这样能够反映中国的传统婚俗。"磕头作揖"是中国的旧时礼节,表示的是对长辈的尊敬,此处将其直译为"kowtow and bow"。

> ……钱麻子的老婆两个搀亲。到晚,一乘轿子、四对灯笼火把,娶进门来。进房撒帐,说四言八句,拜花烛,吃交杯盏,不必细说。
>
> （吴敬梓《儒林外史》）
>
> ...Pork—marked Qian's wife to escort the bride to the house. Towards evening the bridal chair arrived, with your pairs of lanterns and torches. The bride and groom went to the marriage chamber, recited usual phrases, bowed before the decorated candles, drank wine together, and all the rest of it.
>
> （杨宪益　戴乃迭 译）

"搀亲"在旧时指的是婚礼中搀扶新娘下轿,因此译者将其释译为"escort the bride"。"拜花烛""吃交杯盏"是旧时婚礼的习俗,此处译者将其进行了直译,能够很好地保留中国的传统婚俗文化,因此译为"bowed before the decorated candles, drank wine together"。

> 到得二七过了,范举人念旧,拿了几两银子,交与胡屠夫,托他仍旧到集上庵里请平日相与的和尚……
>
> （吴敬梓《儒林外史》）

> When the second seventh day had passed, Fan Jin gave his father-in-law a few taels of silver and told him to go to the temple in the market…
>
> Note: Chinese Buddhists believe that until seven, twice seven or as many as seven times seven days after death does a spirit transmigrate to another body. Thus the masses for a dead person are said within forty-nine days of the death.
>
> （杨宪益　戴乃迭 译）

中国的丧葬文化融合了儒家、道家、佛家的思想理念。"二七"在中国丧葬文化中指的是人死后的第十四天，按照旧时的丧葬习俗，人死后，亲属每七天设斋会奠祭（追荐）一次，前后七次，共四十九天。这一习俗与西方的丧葬习俗完全不一样，因此，外国读者是不明白第二个七天的深层含义的。为了让目的语读者了解中国"做七"的丧葬文化，译者在直译之后加了一定的注解，这样外国读者就会更了解中国的丧葬习俗了。

3. 心理文化与翻译

心理文化会因其所处的社会环境不同而有所差异。人们通过各种感官认识外部世界，通过头脑的活动思考事物之间的因果关系，并伴随着喜、怒、哀、惧等情感体验。在不同的文化背景下，人们的思维方式、道德观、价值观和信仰等存在着较大的差异，这也就导致了人们不同的心理文化。由于心理文化和语言存在着密切的联系，心理文化的差异会直接或者间接地反映在语言的表达习惯上，从而导致语言翻译的障碍。

（1）自谦心理与翻译

谦谦君子，卑以自牧。儒家思想也告诫我们，"三人行，必有我师。"自古以来，在中国社会的人际交往中，人们极为重视"谦虚"，"谦虚"是中国人的美德。古人称自己一方的亲属朋友时，常用"家""舍"等谦辞。"家"是对别人称自己的辈分高或年纪大的亲属时用的谦辞，如家父、家母、家兄等。"舍"用以谦称自己的家或自己的年幼亲属，如寒舍、敝舍、舍弟、舍妹等。在招待客人时，主人会将准备丰盛的饭菜称为"家常便饭"；在展示才华时，表演者则会自称"献丑了"等。

有这样一个笑话：一位外国友人夸赞一名中国女士说，"You are beautiful!"。由于汉语文化中的自谦心理，该女士答道，"Where! Where!（哪里哪里）"，外国友人觉得很困惑，于是回答"Everywhere!"。这只是一则笑话，但是足以见得中西方文化的差异。

汉语文化中的自谦心理会自然而然地反映在语言上,因此,在翻译时需要进行适当的处理,否则会引起目的语读者不必要的误解。

> "他们俩订婚了不多几天,苏老太太来看家母,说了许多好话,说文纨这孩子脾气执拗,她自己劝过女儿没用,还说不要因为这事坏了苏家跟赵家两代交情。"
> （钱钟书《围城》）
>
> "They hadn't been engaged for more than a few days when Mrs. Su came to call on my mother. She was apologetic, mentioning what a stubborn child that Wen-wan was and how she had tried in vain to prevail on Wen-wan, even saying how this might ruin the friendship of two generations between the Su and Chao family."
> （珍妮·凯利 茅国权 译）

"家母"是对别人说自己母亲的谦称,与此同义的还有"家慈"。在翻译时无法在英语中还原其自谦的语用意义,因此直接翻译成所指"my mother"。与其相近的"家父""家严""家君"都是对自己父亲的谦称,可直接翻译成"my father"。

> 贾珍感谢不尽,只说:"待服满后,亲带小犬到府叩谢。"于是作别。
> （曹雪芹《红楼梦》）
>
> Jia Zhen thanked him warmly and promised, "When the mourning is over, I shall bring my worthless son to kowtow his thanks." And so they parted.
> （杨宪益 戴乃迭 译）

"小犬"是一种谦辞,类似的说法还有"犬子"。此处进行了意译,将"小犬"的自谦文化内涵"worthless"翻译了出来。

> "这是我亲戚周太太,敝银行的总经理夫人。你表姐在我出门刚来过电话,所以周太太以为又是她打的。"
> （钱钟书《围城》）
>
> "That's my relative, Mrs. Chou, the wife of the general manager of the bank where I work. Your cousin had called just before I left the house, so Mrs. Chou thought the call was from her again."
> （珍妮·凯利 茅国权 译）

"敝"是一种谦辞,用于跟自己有关的事物。此处"敝银行"指的是说话者自己的工作单位,因此,此处进行了意译,将其译为"the bank where I work"。

> 如海道:"天缘凑巧,因贱荆去世,都中家岳母念及小女无人依傍,前已遣了男女船只来接,因小女未曾大痊,故尚未行,此刻正思送女进京。"
>
> (曹雪芹《红楼梦》)
>
> "What a lucky coincidence!" exclaimed Ju-hai. "Since my wife's death my mother-in-law in the capital has been worried because my daughter has no one to bring her up. She has sent two boats with male and female attendants to fetch the child, but I delayed her departure while she was unwell…"
>
> (杨宪益 戴乃迭 译)

"贱荆"是对自己妻子的谦称,又谦称荆人、荆室、荆妇、拙荆、山荆等。此处不宜将"贱"翻译出来,因此将其意译为"my wife"。同样,"小女"是对自己女儿的谦称,因此在翻译时,直接将其所指翻译出来即可。

> 如果不向女主人打个招呼,那孔碧霞会伤心的。孔碧霞和她的女儿还在忙着,听说我要走,有点儿扫兴:"啊呀,大概是我做的菜不好吧,不合你的口味!"
>
> (陆文夫《美食家》)
>
> Kong would be very hurt if I didn't say goodbye to her. Kong and her daughter were still busy cooking. When she heard I was leaving, she was disappointed. "Oh, perhaps you don't like my cooking, not to your palate."
>
> (包惠南 译)

此处"大概是我做的菜不好吧"是一种自谦的说法,如果直译的话会造成目的语读者的误解,因此,此处译者将其进行了意译,将主语变成了"you",将自谦语的内在含义翻译出来,避免了不必要的误解。

由此可见,在翻译自谦语时,需要考虑中西方的文化差异,为了避免跨文化交际的障碍,译者需要根据语境选择合适的翻译方法进行翻译,以达到交际的平衡。

(2)价值观念与翻译

人们的价值观念是在特定的时代和社会生活环境中形成的,具有相对稳定和持久性的特征,是指导人们为人处世的价值标准。作为心理文化的重要组成部分,价值观念"告诉人们什么行为是社会所期望的,什么是社会所唾弃的,应该爱什么恨什么;什么是美的,什么是好的;什么是丑的,什么是坏的;什么是正常的,什么是荒谬的;什么是正义的,什么是非正义的"(贾雨新,1998)。

中国人的价值观念与儒家思想紧密相连,儒家倡导的是"仁、义、礼、智、信"。孔子曰:"仁者,人也,亲亲为大;义者,宜也,尊贤为大;亲亲之杀,尊贤之等,礼所生也。"孟子曰:"仁之实,事亲是也;义之实,从兄是也;智之实,知斯二者弗去(背离)是也。礼之实,节文斯二者是也"。在儒家思想的影响下,中国人重仁爱、守孝悌、有礼仪、讲尊卑。此外,中国人崇尚无私奉献,爱国主义、集体主义精神深入人心。而西方的价值观念主要表现在重视个体、顺应人性、严格规范等。由此可见,中国人的价值观念与西方崇尚的价值观念存在一定的差异。

语言作为文化的载体,传递着人们的价值观念。因此,在进行中国文化外译的时候,需要充分考虑不同文化价值观念的差异性,选择合理的方法进行翻译。例如,"断子绝孙"在汉语中是一句骂人的话,是一种诅咒。在中国的传统道德观念中,"不孝有三,无后为大",因为没有子孙后代就意味着家族的衰败。在翻译时不可仅仅翻译为"die without sons or grandsons",而应该添加一定的注解"a curse intolerable to hear in China"(包惠南,2004)。

价值观念具有强烈的文化特点,汉语中体现价值观念的词语或者句子承载了特定的人生观和世界观。在翻译的过程中应该根据源语的社会语境及文化语境来确定适当的翻译方法,具体而言,与价值观念相关的文本在翻译时可采用改译、意译和加注的方法。

> 州县官儿虽小,事情却大,为那一州的州官,就是那<u>一方的父母</u>。你不安分守己,尽忠报国,孝敬主子,只怕天也不容你。
>
> (曹雪芹《红楼梦》)
>
> A district magistrate may not rank too high yet he has a lot of work to do as <u>the father and mother of everyone in the district</u>. If you don't behave properly as a loyal servant of the state to be worthy of your masters' kindness, Heaven and Earth will surely condemn you.
>
> (杨宪益 戴乃迭 译)

在封建社会,父母是子女的主宰,同时父母又最疼爱自己的子女,所以"父母官"就兼具了领导与爱护的特点,一个好的地方官应该像爱护子女一样爱护百姓,这就是"爱民如子"。在这个语境中,"一方父母"指的是当地民众的"父母官",反映了中国的价值观念,即"仁爱"。此处宜采用意译的方式将"一方父母"的真正内涵传递给目的语读者。

(3) 审美心理与翻译

审美心理(aesthetic psychology)是指人对客观对象的美的主观反映。人的审美心理产生于人类的生产和社会生活实践,并在长期历史进程中逐渐发展、丰富和完善,因此具有一定的文化特点。汉语受华夏文化传统思维和审美心理的影响,长期以来形成了独特的艺术魅力:以意统形、概括灵活、言简意丰、音韵和谐。这些特点互相融合,体现在汉语的各个层次,深深融入中国人的审美情趣之中(李申,1998)。

审美心理在语言上主要表现在韵律、词汇、修辞等方面。韵律方面,汉语中叠音词、拟声词比较常见,如"无边落木萧萧下,不尽长江滚滚来。""弯弯的月儿小小的船,小小的船儿两头尖。我在小小的船里坐,只看见,闪闪的星星蓝蓝的天。"修辞方面,汉语喜用比喻、拟人、排比、夸张、重复等修辞手法,如"叶子出水很高,像亭亭的舞女的裙。层层的叶子中间,零星地点缀着些白花,有袅娜地开着的,有羞涩地打着朵儿的;正如一粒粒的明珠,又如碧天里的星星,又如刚出浴的美人。"词汇层面,汉语中四字结构很多,辞藻华丽,描述生动形象。相比之下,英语主张简洁客观。

由于翻译是一种跨文化的活动,因此,译者需要熟悉源语和译语的审美心理差异,进而了解由于审美心理差异造成的语言上的差异。例如"但我的事现在搞得满城风雨,人人皆知了。"其中,"满城风雨""人人皆知"在该句中表述的意思是一样的,在翻译时对语义重复的部分可以进行删减,将二者的意思翻译出来即可,无须重复强调。由此,可以将其译为"But there had been too much publicity about my case."。由此可见,译者在翻译时需要充分考虑由审美导致的语言差异,这样才能译出符合目的语读者审美心理的成功译文。

"眼前的一切：闪闪发光的桥梁、浊水翻滚的河流、密密麻麻的灌木、惊慌失措的燕子、呆若木鸡的妹妹们……"

(莫言《丰乳肥臀》)

"The scene arrayed before her—the sun glinting off the bridge beams, the churning, muddy river, densely packed shrubbery, all the startled swallows and her stunned sisters…"

(葛浩文 译)

此处原文中有多个四字结构，既有叠字又有成语，在汉语原文中起到了平衡文本的作用。如若将其逐字翻译，译文中会有很多定语成分，其中"呆若木鸡的妹妹们"还要使用定语从句，译文就会累赘冗余，因此，译者进行了意译。"闪闪发光的桥梁"转换成目的语时将主语由原来的桥梁变成了"the sun"，放在该语境下更符合目的语读者的审美心理。同时，其余的四字结构分别用简洁明了的形容词进行了翻译，译文整体更加简练。

各级政府都要节用为民、坚持过紧日子，确保基本民生支出只增不减，助力市场主体青山常在、生机盎然。

(2021年政府工作报告)

We at every level of government should practice fiscal frugality in the interests of the people. We should continue to tighten our belts, ensure continued increases in spending to meet basic living needs, and help sustain and energize market entities.

(https://language.chinadaily.com.cn/a/202103/15/WS604ed1cfa31024adobaaf337.html)

此处的"青山常在"和"生机盎然"是四字结构，在该语境中均指让市场主体能够一直存在并具有活力。因此，译者对其进行了意译。

江岸上彩楼林立，彩灯高悬，旌旗飘摇，呈现出一派喜气洋洋的节日场面。千姿百态的各式彩龙在江面上游弋，舒展着优美的身姿，有的摇头摆尾，风采奕奕；有的喷火吐水，威风八面。

(何志范《乐山龙舟会多姿多彩》)

> High-rise buildings or ornamented with colored lanterns and bright banners stand out along the river banks. On the river itself, gaily decorated dragon-shaped boats await their challenge, displaying their individual charms to their hearts' content. One boat wags its head and tail; another spits fire and sprays water.
>
> （包惠南 译）

该汉语原文中包含多个四字结构，表意精当，读来朗朗上口。但是，如果对其进行直译，会使译文修饰语过多，造成译文的冗长与拖沓，且不符合目的语的阅读习惯。因此，考虑到源语读者与目的语读者不同的审美心理，译者对其进行了省译，将一些在译文中起不到语用作用的词句删掉未译。由此得出的译文简洁明了，同时又再现了喜气洋洋的场面。

由此可见，译者在处理审美心理差异的问题时，往往采用意译及省译的方式来达到跨语言、跨文化交际的成功。

（4）思维方式与翻译

人们的思维方式是在长期的社会生活中逐渐形成的，不同文化的人们，生活的环境既有共性又有个性，因此，不同文化的人们的思维方式也既有共同点又有不同点。中国人的思维方式大多偏向于具象思维、综合型思维、本体型思维和顺向思维；而西方人的思维方式大多偏向于抽象思维、分析型思维、客体型思维和逆向型思维。思维方式的差异导致了人们语言表达方式的不同。

汉语句子多取线性结构，即各分句平行并列，不分主次；英语句子多取分层结构，即各分句环环相扣，主次分明。英语句子讲究形式美，结构繁复，以长句居多；汉语则注重内在语意连贯，以意统形，以短句为主。在进行汉英翻译时需要适当的调整句子结构以符合目的语读者的思维方式。

①分译

汉语句子结构相对松散，短句子较多，类似"大江流水，后浪推前浪"。这种流水似的句式在进行英译时需要译者根据意群断句，将原句拆分成两个或多个句子并用逻辑连接词将其串联起来。

> （鲁智深）先把戒刀和包裹拴了,<u>往下丢落去</u>;又把禅杖也撺落去;却把身<u>往下只一滚</u>,骨碌碌直滚到山脚边,并无伤损,跳将起来,寻了包裹,跨了戒刀,拿了禅杖,拽开脚步,取路便走。
>
> （施耐庵《水浒传》）
>
> He tied the sack and knife together, <u>dropped them over the side</u>, and tossed the staff down after them. Then he <u>rolled down the slope</u>, tumbling all the way to the foot of the mountain without injury.
>
> （沙博理 译）

原文由十二个短句子构成,译者将其改为两个长句:第一句描述鲁智深在滚下山前的一系列动作;第二句描述鲁智深从山上滚下去之后的行为。两个句子之间由"then"连接,表示动作发生的前后顺序。相比于原文。译文的时间顺序更加明了,更符合目的语读者的思维方式。

> 各地区各部门顾全大局、尽责担当,上亿市场主体在应对冲击中展现出坚强韧性,广大人民群众勤劳付出、共克时艰,诠释了百折不挠的民族精神,彰显了人民是真正的英雄,这是我们战胜一切困难挑战的力量源泉。
>
> （2021年政府工作报告）
>
> Yet, local authorities and government departments across the country kept in mind the big picture and shouldered their responsibilities. Market entities, over one hundred million in number, responded to shocks with fortitude and resilience. Our people worked hard and fought adversity in close solidarity and with the unyielding spirit of the Chinese nation, thus proving themselves true heroes. This is the well of strength that enables us to rise to every challenge and overcome every difficulty.
>
> （https://language.chinadaily.com.cn/a/202103/15/WS604ed1cfa31024ad0baaf337.html）

原文由六个短句构成,分为四个意群,四个主语分别是"各地区各部门""市场主体""人民群众"和"这",因此译者将其分译为四个句子,使译文一目了然。

> 在中共中央和中央军委的坚强领导下,西安"八办"同志肩负重托,不辱使命,完成党中央赋予的"建立秘密联络交通,开展隐蔽战线斗争,营救失散红军战士"等多项任务,为中华民族的独立与解放作出了重要贡献。
>
> Under the leadership of the CPC Central Committee and the CPC Military Commission, leaders and staff of the ERAXO made important contributions to the independence and liberation of the Chinese nation by fulfilling various tasks given by the CPC Central Committee. Those tasks were to set up a secret contact point, carry out the underground struggle, rescue scattered soldiers and commanders.
>
> (八路军西安办事处)

原文的句子,看似形式松散,但是形散意合。在翻译成英语的过程中,如果完全照搬原文的句子结构,译文会显得冗长且部分无主语。因此,译者采用了分译的方法,将原文拆分成两个句子,既传达了原文的意思,又让句子结构看起来更合理。

②**合译**

汉语重语义结构,多有言外之意的超文本特性,强调情景上的意蕴对接;英语重句法结构,多用关联句法,讲究语法内在逻辑关系。汉译英时要根据情况利用连词、介词、不定式、定语从句、独立结构等把汉语短句连成长句。翻译时,遇到几个主语重复、代词复指、逻辑或意思紧密的汉语短句时,既可以将其合译为一个主从句,也可将其合译为成分较为复杂的简单句。其优点不仅在于用词不多,而且译文的逻辑关系也更加明显,更符合英文的表达习惯。

> 直到1978年党的十一届三中全会后,在以邓小平同志为核心的党中央领导下,我们党终于找到了一条建设有中国特色的社会主义道路。这条道路被概括为"一个中心、两个基本点"。这是一条坚持马克思列宁主义的社会主义原理,一切从实际出发的道路。
>
> (胡乔木《中国共产党的七十年》)

> Not until the 3rd Plenary Session of the 11th CPC Central Committee held in 1978 could the Chinese Communist Party, under the leadership of its Central Committee with Deng Xiaoping at the core, finally find a road for socialist construction with Chinese characteristics, <u>which is generalized as having one central task and two basic points and which is also a road adhering to the principles of Marxism and Leninism on socialism and proceeding from the reality in everything.</u>
>
> (包惠南 译)

汉语原文画线部分的两个句子与其前面一句中的"建设有中国特色的社会主义道路"存在语义逻辑关系。后两句是对"建设有中国特色的社会主义道路"的阐述与说明,因此在进行英译时可将二者处理成非限制性定语从句,把原文的三句话合译为一句话。

练习题

一、将下列词汇翻译成英语,注意其文化内涵。

1. 红利
2. 黑货
3. 灰色收入
4. 双黄线
5. 红榜
6. 红娘
7. 红包
8. 红茶
9. 白酒
10. 黑名单

二、将下列句子翻译成英语。

1. 假洋鬼子回来时,向秀才讨还了四块洋钱,秀才便有一块银桃子挂在大襟上了。(鲁迅《阿Q正传》)

2. 如果出到十几文,那就能买一样荤菜,但这些顾客,多是短衣帮,大抵没有这样阔绰。只有穿长衫的,才踱进店面隔壁的房子里,要酒要菜,慢慢地坐喝。(鲁迅《孔乙己》)

3. 生活在奴才们中间,作奴才们的首领,我将引为生平的最大耻辱,最大的悲哀。(聂绀弩《我若为王》)

4. 母亲突然大笑起来,笑着笑着,流出了一脸泪。我和妻子也流了泪。(张林《大钱饺子》)

5. 我想那就给妻子吧,她跟我生活了 20 年,现在已经是快半百的人了。为了我挨斗,她心血都快要熬干了。(张林《大钱饺子》)

6. 在处理与师父、同门及他人的关系时,应当谦虚、诚信、知礼、仁义。

7. 中国人的祖先在那时已经使用鼎、大釜、蒸笼等烹制食物。

8. 倒是我们家大媳妇的两个堂妹子生得人才齐整,二姑娘已经许了人家,三姑娘正好与令郎为配。(曹雪芹《红楼梦》)

9. 近来家母偶着了些风寒,不好了两天。(曹雪芹《红楼梦》)

10. "王大人说哪里话,你我两家又不是初交。再说,舍妹专门嘱咐我,务请大人屈尊,小妹要谈的是闺门夫婿之事,我当哥哥的也不好在旁。"

三、将下列段落翻译成英语。

我家的后面有一个很大的园,相传叫作百草园。现在是早已并屋子一起卖给朱文公的子孙了,连那最末次的相见也已经隔了七八年,其中似乎确凿只有一些野草;但那时却是我的乐园。

不必说碧绿的菜畦,光滑的石井栏,高大的皂荚树,紫红的桑椹;也不必说鸣蝉在树叶里长吟,肥胖的黄蜂伏在菜花上,轻捷的叫天子(云雀)忽然从草间直窜向云霄里去了。单是周围的短短的泥墙根一带,就有无限趣味。油蛉在这里低唱,蟋蟀们在这里弹琴。翻开断砖来,有时会遇见蜈蚣;还有斑蝥,倘若用手指按住它的脊梁,便会"拍"的一声,从后窍喷出一阵烟雾。(鲁迅《从百草园到三味书屋》)

第四章 专有名词的翻译

专有名词是指人名、地名、机构团体名和其他具有特殊含义的名词或名词词组。中西方在物质文化、精神文化等方面存在巨大差异,而专有名词是对一个社会客观事物、社会现象及意识概念等内容的命名,往往为一个社会及一种语言所特有,因此译者常常在另一种语言中找不到对应概念及语言表达形式。例如,道家学说的核心概念——"道"。"道"是世界的最高真理,"道"是宇宙万物的本源,将"道"译作"the way"或者音译为"Tao"都很难反映其丰富的哲学内涵。专有名词的翻译并非易事,译者需要掌握一定的原则与策略,才能在英语中再现具有文化特色的专有名词,促进中西文化交流。

1. 人名翻译

人名蕴含着丰富的内涵意义,体现着父母对孩子的期望与祝愿,有些名字结合五行及生肖,则更具文化特色。人名翻译最常见的方法是音译,如"陈白露""李白""谭招弟"可译作"Chen Bailu""Li Bai""Tan Zhaodi"。这符合我国 2001 年 1 月 1 日起开始实施的《国家通用语言文字法》中的第十八条规定,即"国家通用语言文字以《汉语拼音方案》作为人名拼写和注音的工具。"这种翻译方法方便操作,能够让英语读者感受到人名的异国气息。但音译人名也存在一些问题,因为人名所承载的殷切期望经过音译后荡然无存。例如"解放""伟业""玉洁""秀丽",在汉语中的象征意义分别是"国家解放""伟大事业""冰清玉洁"及"灵秀美丽",但音译为"Jiefang""Weiye""Yujie""Xiuli"后,大多数英语读者都不知道这些名字的含义。因此,英译汉语人名时,译者可采用音译加注解的方式进行翻译,以再现人名所承载的象征意义。

> 钱先生周岁时"抓周",抓了一本书,因此得名"钟书"。
>
> When Qian was just one year old, he was told by his parents to choose one thing among many things, he picked up a book of all things. Thereupon his father very gladly gave him the name:Zhongshu (book lover).
>
> (陈宏薇《新实用汉译英教程》)

> 徐霞客(1587—1641),名宏祖,字振之,号霞客,又号霞逸,江阴(今属江苏)人。他的好友陈继儒因他酷爱旅行,经常餐霞宿露于山林野泽之间,为他取名"霞客"。
>
> Xu Xiake (1587—1641), whose given name is "Hongzu" and who styled himself as "Zhenzhi," "Xiake," "Xiayi," was a native of Jiangyin (present in Jiangsu Province). As he was very interested in travelling and liked to spend the night outdoors to savor the dew and enjoy the first morning rays, his friend Chen Jiru named him "Xiake", the guest of the morning ray.
>
> (陈宏薇《高级汉英翻译》)

> 这小子无名无姓,左脸上有巴掌大的一块蓝痣,我随口说,你小子就叫蓝脸吧,姓蓝名脸。
>
> The boy had no name, but since he had a blue birthmark on the left side of his face, I told him I'd call him Lan Lian or Blue Face, with Lan being his surname.
>
> (葛浩文 译)

有些人名已经被翻译成英语,而且已沿用多年,如孙中山(Sun Yat-sen)、蒋介石(Chiang Kai-shek)、孔子(Confucius)、孟子(Mencius)沿用约定俗成的译名即可。

2. 地名翻译

中华文化常常赋予地名特殊的含义,在地名中可以解读出特有的历史文化、民间传说或地理特征,如"卧佛沟""龙桥沟""惊驾村""梁家河"等。翻译汉语地名的一般原则为音译,这一翻译方法有利于外国人在中国境内交际。与"Daqing Road"相比"Daqinglu",在中国的交际效果就更好一些。因此,音译地名具有重要的实用意义。

如果是英语读者，音译就显得不足，因为音译不能再现汉语地名内涵的民族性、时代性与社会性，甚至连基本行政单位或实指概念都无法表达清楚。如将"惊驾村"音译为"Jingjiacun"，英语读者恐怕无法理解"cun"其实指的是"village"。因此，地名也可采用音译加直译的方法，将专名部分用汉语拼音，通用名部分译为"Ave.""Rd.""St""District""County""City""Province"等，如"长寿区""灵宝市"可分别翻译为"Changshou District""Lingbao City"。如果专名和通用名词均为单音节，英译时可将通用名视作专名的一部分，再重复翻译通用名，如"洋县""滦镇"可译为"Yangxian County""Luanzhen Town"。地名体现着民族尊严，象征着领土主权，无论是音译还是音译加意译都能够直观地体现地名所负载的这一政治内涵。另外，翻译我国行政地区时需参考有关书籍或词典，以保证译名的统一性及严肃性。

山川湖泊名称作为地名的一部分，音译加直译是最为常见的翻译方法。如果专有名词和通用名词均为单音节，英译时可将通用名译为专名的一部分，并重复翻译通用名词。如"华山""泰山""崂山""湘江""岷江""太湖"可分别译为"Huashan Mountain/Mount Huashan""Taishan Mountain/Mount Taishan""Laoshan Mountain/Mount Laoshan""Xiangjiang River""Minjiang River""Taihu Lake"。同时，汉语的"山"可根据实际海拔高度、地理位置、地貌特征、历史文化等信息灵活翻译为"Mountains""Mount""Range""Rock"或"Peak"。如"秦岭""天山""太行山""阴山""惠山"分别译为"the Qinling Mountains""the Tianshan Mountains""the Taihang Range""the Yinshan Mountains""Huishan Hill"。有一些地名已经有固定的英语表达形式，采用约定俗成的译名即可，如"香山""黄河""长江""西湖"可译为"Fragrant Hill""the Yellow River""the Yangtze River""the West Lake"。

3. 文化术语翻译

文化术语是特定领域内承载概念的词或词组，准确自然的文化术语翻译在中外交流与中华文化传播中发挥着重要作用。文化术语不同于普通术语，除兼具普通术语准确性、简洁性、稳定性的特点外，文化术语扎根于中华文明五千年悠久的历史文化土壤中，是中华民族社会生活、宗教信仰、经济民生、伦理道德的体现，其翻译往往更具挑战。文化通常可分为物质文化、制度文化及精神文化三大类。文化术语作为表征文化概念的语言符号,其语义概念的复杂性不言而喻,尤其是精神文化术语。物质文化术语的概念客体常常以物质形态呈现,如尊、鼎、深衣、辈子、斗拱、脸谱、埙、琵琶、茶楼、元宵等,这些指称客观物体的术语涉及我们生活的方方面面;制度文化术语以抽象体制形态呈现,如八股文、包干到户、农转非、中国特色社会主义、西部大开发、"一带一路"倡议等能够反映国家行政管理体制、人才培养选拔制度、法律制度和民间的礼仪俗规等内容;精神文化术语往往更具抽象性,反映着一个民族的价值观念、道德规范、心理素质、精神面貌、行为准则、审美观念,如仁义礼智信、天人合一、无为、居安思危、上善若水等。文化术语浓缩了中华民族的社会历史、哲学思想、价值观念,是中华民族智慧的结晶。

文化术语翻译的重点在于文化概念的跨语境表达,离开中华文化土壤,在英语文化的语境下再现中华文化概念。在这一过程中,译者应确保术语翻译的准确性、简明性及稳定性。音译是文化术语翻译中常见的翻译方法,如纳吉(Naji)、阴阳(Yin Yang)、功夫(Gongfu)、乾(Qian)、坤(Kun)等。音译文化术语能够有效保留源语的异域气息,而且语境或配图能够帮助音译准确再现源语所承载的文化信息,不失为一种简明有效的翻译方法。但如果上下文解释不够,或配图不到位,并且读者的文化预设不充分,音译则不能有效传达源语文化概念,翻译简而不明。

为了弥补音译的不足,音译加直译也是一种有效的翻译方法,如仁[Ren(Humanness)]、[义 Yi (Righteousness)]、礼[Li (Propriety)]、智[Zhi(Wisdom)]、信[Xin (Trustworthy and Reliability)]、无为[Wuwei (Non-action)]。虽然括号中的内容并没有完全精准再现源语丰富的文化内涵,但与仅仅使用音译的方法相比,这一翻译方法既保留了源语的语言特色又传达了源语的语义概念,不失为一种有效的翻译方法。

有些文化术语的内涵意义十分丰富,并且在译入语中没有对应的词汇表达,这时使用音译加意译的翻译方法可以在保留汉语词汇特质的基础上,较为准确地表达源语的文化内涵。如中庸[Zhongyong (golden mean)]、火候[Huohou (length of cooking and temperature)]、中和[Zhonghe(social harmony)]、工笔画[gongbi (flower-and-bird) paintings]。但这一方法的不足也十分明显,音译加意译的翻译方法使译文不够简洁,很难给读者带来与源语读者相同的阅读感受。

此外,直译也是文化术语常用的翻译方法之一,如德性(sense of virtue)、甲骨文（oracle bone inscriptions）、丝绸之路（the Silk Road）、中国结（Chinese knots）、科学发展观（the Outlook of Scientific Development）、药膳（medical diet）、药酒（medicated wine）、腰鼓（waist drum）、月饼（moon cake）、龙舟（dragon boat）等。这一翻译方法保留了汉语文化术语的简明性及形象性，但这一方法也有很大的局限性，没有深入词汇的文化内涵，需要译入语读者具备相关的文化预设。

增译也是一种常见的翻译方法。增译是指根据两种语言不同的文化背景、语言习惯及表达方式，在翻译时添加解释性短语或句子，以准确再现源语文化信息，消除译入语读者的困惑与误解，从而优化翻译效果，实现文化移植的目的。如元宵（sweet dumplings made of glutinous rice）、粽子（pyramid-shaped dumplings made of glutinous rice wrapped in bamboo or reed leaves）、八卦[the Eight Trigrams（eight combinations of three lines—all solid, all broken, or a combination of solid and broken lines—joined in pairs to form 64 hexagrams, formerly used in divination）]。增补注解后，"八卦"的文化内涵十分明确，确保了译文读者对该文化术语的透彻理解。又如"八股文"也可增译为"eight-part essay（a literary composition prescribed for the imperial civil service examinations, known for its rigidity of form and poverty of ideas）"，"满月酒"可增译为"One-month-old Birthday Feast（a special ceremony held after a baby has been one month old）"，等等。除了以括号或注释的形式增译外，文内加注也可以对词语的文化意义进行补充说明。

最后，意译这一常用的翻译方法也可用于翻译文化术语，如五行（Five Elements）、压岁钱（New Year Money）、凉茶（herbal tea）、六君子汤（Decoction Containing Six Mild Drugs）、皮蛋（preserved egg）、相声（Chinese cross-talk）。这一翻译方法语言表达简明，充分照顾到译入语读者文化预设不足的情况，不会产生歧义，方便译入语读者阅读理解。但这一翻译方法没有考虑源语语言形式，欠缺文化色彩。

文化术语的翻译是一个复杂的过程，译者需考虑方方面面的因素，如源语的表达形式、术语文化内涵、译入语文化、译入语表达规范、译入语读者文化预设及翻译类型等。无论哪种翻译方法，目的都是要忠实准确地传达汉语词语的文化内涵，克服文化差异的障碍，促进汉英文化之间的交流，在两种文化间搭起沟通的桥梁。

练习题

一、翻译下列内容，并讨论使用的术语翻译方法。

1. 孝
2. 不争
3. 无为而治
4. 太极
5. 京剧
6. 春卷
7. 剪纸
8. 对联
9. 号脉
10. 草书
11. 太庙
12. 刮痧
13. 元宵节
14. 唐三彩
15. 毛泽东思想
16. 三纲
17. 五常
18. 文房四宝
19. 满月酒
20. 龙虎斗

二、翻译下列句子。

1. 这两个女孩，长名互助，幼名合作。他们姓黄，是黄瞳的种子。

2. 第二年初春她就生了龙凤胎，男名西门金龙，女名西门宝凤。

3. 中国结是中国最为流行的传统民间艺术形式之一，最初是由手工艺人发明的，经过数百年的不断改进，已经成为一门优雅的艺术。

4. 京剧是中国最受欢迎、影响最大的剧种，被认为是中国的"国剧"，至今已有两百多年历史。

5. 中国古代建筑注重等级秩序，住房讲究尊卑长幼。

第五章 习语与翻译

习语汇聚了语言的精华,而语言是文化的载体。因此,习语的语言也是文化的载体。习语包括成语、俗语、格言、歇后语、谚语、俚语、典故、行话等,往往比较简洁明了,又生动形象。习语反映了不同地区、不同民族的文化特色,因此要了解习语的意义就要具备相应的文化背景知识。

习语的翻译不仅要考虑源语习语的寓意,还要考虑译语接受群体的民族特色、接受心理和表达习惯(包惠南,2004),只有这样才能够让译语充分体现源语的文化特色。因此,有效传递习语的文化信息是习语翻译的重中之重。

1. 汉语成语的翻译

成语(set phrases)是"人们长期以来习用的、简洁精辟的定型词组或短句。汉语的成语大多由四个字组成,一般都有出处"(《现代汉语词典》)。有些成语从字面上不难理解,如"助人为乐""念念不忘""风和日丽"等。有些成语必须知道来源或典故才能懂得意思,如"沉鱼落雁""坐井观天""滴水穿石""掩耳盗铃""杯弓蛇影"等。汉语成语结构比较稳定,历史悠久,寓意深刻,且许多成语都源于故事。汉语成语的翻译可以采用多种翻译方法,如直译、直译兼意译、意译、套译等。

(1)直译

为了保留汉语成语的文化特色,让目的语读者了解中国的语言文化与魅力,译者在翻译汉语成语的时候可以进行直译。直译最大限度地保留了源语的原汁原味。

> 林黛玉笑道:"你说你会过目成诵,难道我就不能一目十行了?"
>
> (曹雪芹《红楼梦》)
>
> "You boast that you can memorize a passage with one reading! Why can't I learn ten lines at a glance?"
>
> (杨宪益 戴乃迭 译)

"一目十行"出自《梁书·简文帝纪》"读书十行俱下",意思是看书时同时可以看十行。这个成语常用于形容看书非常快,可延伸出聪明伶俐、善于总结的意思。此处译者为了还原源语的文化特色,对其进行了直译,很好地传达了源语的文化内涵。

> 薛蝌说:"大哥哥这几年在外头相与的都是些什么人,连一个正经的也没有,来一起子,都是些狐群狗党。"
>
> (曹雪芹《红楼梦》)
>
> "The friends Brother Pan has been making these years!" he fumed. "There's not a single decent sort among the whole foxy lot. They're a park of curs.
>
> (杨宪益 戴乃迭 译)

"狐群狗党"出自《气英布》第四折,"咱若不是扶刘锄项,逐着那狐群狗党,兀良怎显得咱这黥面当王!",比喻勾结在一起的坏人。此处译者将"狐群"译为了"the whole foxy lot",将"狗党"译为了"a park of curs",其中"狗"选择了"cur"(恶狗)这一形象的词语,生动地还原了源语中的文化喻体。

> 陈达叫将起来,说道:"你两个闭了鸟嘴!长别人志气,灭自己威风!他只是一个人,须不三头六臂,我不信。"
>
> (施耐庵 罗贯中《水浒传》)
>
> "Shut your craven mouths," Chen Da cried. "Praising other people's courage pulls down your own. After all he's only human. Does he have three heads and six arms? I don't believe it!"
>
> (沙博理 译)

"三头六臂"出自释道原《景德传灯录·普昭禅师》,"三头六臂擎天地,愤怒哪吒扑帝钟。"意思是三个脑袋,六条胳膊;原指佛的法相,后比喻神奇的本领。此处译者直译之后,目的语读者能够理解其内在含义,一个长着三个头、六个胳膊的人,一定是具有超凡本领的,源语的文化形象通过直译得以生动地再现。

> "家里粗茶淡饭的苦生活,你也应该过过……"
> 　　　　　　　　　　　　　　　　　　　　　　(钱钟书《围城》)
> "You should put up with the hard life of 'coarse tea and plain rice'…"
> 　　　　　　　　　　　　　　(Jeanne Kelly and Mao Nathan K. 译)

"粗茶淡饭"出自黄庭坚《四休导士诗序》:"粗茶淡饭饱即休,补破遮寒暖即休,三平二满过即休,不贪不妒老即休。",指粗糙简单的饮食。此处译者同样对其进行了直译。

> 现在呢,她高高在上,跟自己的地位简直是云泥之别。
> 　　　　　　　　　　　　　　　　　　　　　　(钱钟书《围城》)
> Now she was as high above him as the clouds were from the mud.
> 　　　　　　　　　　　　　　　　　　(珍妮·凯利　茅国权 译)

"云泥之别"出自荀济《赠阴梁州》,"云泥已殊路",意思是像天上的云和地上的泥那样高下不同,比喻地位的高低相差极大。译者保留了源语中的两个意象:云和泥,将其进行了直译。目的语读者在此语境中可以理解云和泥之间的差距,也就能够理解此处的寓意了。

> 叫一声:"请!"一齐举箸,却如风卷残云一般,早去了一半。
> 　　　　　　　　　　　　　　　　　　　　　(吴敬梓《儒林外史》)
> At the signal to begin, they fell to with their chopsticks, like a whirlwind scattering wisps of cloud.
> 　　　　　　　　　　　　　　　　　　　　　(杨宪益　戴乃迭 译)

"风卷残云"意思是大风把残云卷走,比喻一下子把残存的东西一扫而光。译者此处用直译保留了成语中的"风"和"残云",非常形象地在译文中再现了几人吃饭的情形。

(2) 意译

汉语成语蕴含了丰富的文化意义,如果没有将成语的内在含义翻译出来,有可能会导致交际的失败。因此,译者可以采用意译的方法传达其中的文化内涵。

> 他自然吓得要死,而那老和尚却道无妨,给他一个小盒子,说只要放在枕边,便可高枕而卧。
>
> (鲁迅《朝花夕拾》)
>
> The scholar was nearly frightened to death, of course, but the old monk told him not to worry and gave him a little box, assuring him that if he put this by his pillow he could go to sleep without fear.
>
> (杨宪益 戴乃迭 译)

"高枕而卧"的字面意思是垫高枕头安心地睡觉,形容人无忧无虑、平安无事。此处如果采用直译的方法,目的语读者将不能理解其真正的含义。通过意译可以成功地向目的语读者传达原文的含义,进而避免理解上的障碍。

> 宝玉听了,如醍醐灌顶,"哎哟"了一声,方笑道:"怪道我们家庙说是'铁槛寺'呢!原来有此一说。"
>
> (曹雪芹《红楼梦》)
>
> Baoyu felt as if Buddha had suddenly shown him the light. "Aiya!" he exclaimed. "No wonder our family temple is called Iron Threshold Temple. So that's the origin of the name."
>
> (杨宪益 戴乃迭 译)

佛家以"醍醐灌顶"比喻灌输智慧,使人得到启发,彻底醒悟,也比喻听了高明的意见使人受到很大启发。"醍醐"原指酥酪上凝聚的油,如果将该成语进行直译的话,目的语读者会很费解,因此,为了传达该成语的内涵,译者采用了意译的方法,在该语境将其译为"Buddha had suddenly shown him the light"。

> "惩治?"相如傲然一笑道:"想我司马相如学富五车,却只能站在宫门之前,还要像被耍的猢狲一样任人摆布,这事我早就不想干了!"
>
> (徐飞《凤求凰》)
>
> "Severe punishment?" scoffed Xiangru. "Do you think a man of my education is good only for standing in doorways being ordered about prancing monkeys like those fellows? I never wanted this job in the first place!"
>
> (保罗·怀特 译)

"学富五车"出自《庄子·天下》,"惠施多方,其书五车",意思是学问渊博。同样,为了避免直译给目的语读者带来误解,译者在此处采用了意译。

> 季苇萧道:"先生大名,如雷贯耳。小弟献丑,真是弄斧班门了。"
>
> (吴敬梓《儒林外史》)
>
> "Your great fame long since reached my ears like thunder," responded Ji. "I am ashamed to display my incompetence before a connoisseur like yourself."
>
> (杨宪益 戴乃迭 译)

"弄斧班门"出自柳宗元的《王氏伯仲唱和诗序》,"操斧于班、郢之门,斯强颜耳",意思是在鲁班门前舞弄斧子,比喻在行家面前卖弄本领,不自量力。此处译者采用了意译,将其翻译成"display my incompetence before a connoisseur",准确传达了成语的寓意所在。

> 梁山伯肃然说:"贤弟放心!'君子一言,驷马难追'。不过,若是伯父母不肯允婚呢?"
>
> (赵清阁《梁山伯与祝英台》)
>
> Liang Shanbo spoke solemnly, "Don't worry, you have the word of a gentleman, and a gentleman always honors his word. But what if your parents don't agree to this marriage?"
>
> (托马斯 译)

"君子一言,驷马难追"出自《论语·颜渊》,"夫子之说君子也,驷不及舌",意思是一句话说出了口,就是套上四匹马拉的车也难追上。这句话常用在承诺之后,表示说话算数。因为目的语读者并不了解其来源和寓意,此处译者没有直译"驷马难追",而是采用了意译的方法,方便目的语读者明白"驷马难追"的意思。

> 除了平儿,众丫头媳妇无不言三语四,指桑说槐,暗相讥讽。
>
> (曹雪芹《红楼梦》)
>
> All the maids and servants, with the exception of Pinger, kept gossiping, making sarcastic remarks, and casting aspersions at Second Sister.
>
> (杨宪益 戴乃迭 译)

"指桑说槐"的意思是表面上在骂这个人,实际上要骂那个人。在小说中的语境中,它指的是暗地里说别人的闲话,因此译者采用意译,选用了"cast aspersion"这一短语,短语的原意是诽谤,在这个语境中指的是以不实之词诋毁他人。

> 你看这里这些人,因见老太太多疼了宝玉和凤丫头两个,他们尚<u>虎视眈眈</u>,背地里言三语四的,何况于我?
>
> (曹雪芹《红楼梦》)
>
> Look how <u>jealous</u> these people are and how much gossip there is because the old lady favors Baoyu and Xifeng. In my case, they'd resent it even more.
>
> (杨宪益 戴乃迭 译)

"虎视眈眈"出自《周易·颐》,"虎视眈眈,其欲逐逐",意思是像老虎那样凶狠地盯着,形容心怀不善,伺机攫取。在小说的语境当中指的是其他人嫉妒老太太疼爱宠溺宝玉和王熙凤。因此,译者将虎视眈眈进行了意译,译为"jealous"。

> 黛玉听了这个话,不觉将昨晚的事都忘在<u>九霄云外</u>了。
>
> (曹雪芹《红楼梦》)
>
> By now Daiyu's resentment over the previous evening was <u>completely</u> forgotten.
>
> (杨宪益 戴乃迭 译)

"九霄云外"出自《颜氏家训》,"一事惬当,一句清巧,神厉九霄,志凌千载",意思是在九重天的外面,比喻非常遥远的地方或远得无影无踪,在小说中是指黛玉把昨晚的事情完全忘记了。因此译者进行了意译,将其译为"completely"。

(3)直译兼意译

在进行汉语成语翻译的过程中,为了既保留原成语中的文化喻体,又明确成语的比喻意义,译者可以采用直译兼意译的方法。

> 船上站着几个<u>如狼似虎</u>的仆人,手拿鞭子,打那挤河路的船。
>
> (吴敬梓《儒林外史》)
>
> On the deck of this large vessel stood several attendants looking <u>as savage as tigers and wolves</u>, who were lashing out with wisp at all the boats in their way.
>
> (杨宪益 戴乃迭 译)

"如狼似虎"出自《尉缭子·武议》,"一人之兵,如狼似虎,如风如雨,如雷如霆,震震冥冥,天下皆惊",意思是像狼和虎一样凶狠,比喻非常凶暴残忍。为了表达原汉语成语的内涵,译者选用了"savage"一词再现其寓意,同时又保留了原喻体"tigers"和"wolves"。

(4) 套译

由于人类社会的发展具有相似性,因此不同国家的语言和文化也具有一定的相通性。因此,汉语成语与部分英语习语所表示的意思相同或者相近,这时,便可以进行套译,用英语中的习语来翻译汉语中的成语。

健壮如牛	as strong as a horse
害群之马	a black sheep
杀鸡取卵	to kill the goose that lays the golden eggs
血流如注	to bleed like a pig
艳若桃李	as red as rose; like lilies and roses
掌上明珠	apple of somebody's eye
心猿意马	to have a head like a sieve
时不待人	Time and tide wait for no man.
大智若愚	Still waters run deep.
魂飞魄散	to have one's heart in one's mouth
风餐露宿	to cover with moon
声东击西	to shoot at a pigeon and kill a crow
有恃无恐	to count on one's own cards
有条不紊	as regular as clockwork
得不偿失	the game is not worth the candle
花天酒地	to drink the cup of joy
惹是生非	to bring a hornet's nest about one's ears
趁热打铁	to strike while the iron is hot
晴天霹雳	like a bolt from the blue
破釜沉舟	to burn the boat
一箭双雕	to kill two birds with one stone

轻如鸿毛	as light as a feather
骨瘦如柴	as thin as a rail
易如反掌	as easy as turning over one's hand
守口如瓶	as dumb as an oyster
明察秋毫	to see through a brick wall
弱不禁风	as weak as water
出言不逊	to scold like a fish-wife
一清二楚	as clear as crystal
刚愎自用	to harden one's neck
格格不入	a square peg in a round hole
贪得无厌	as greedy as a wolf
画蛇添足	to paint/glid the lily
大海捞针	to look for a needle in a haystack
打草惊蛇	to wake a sleeping dog
雪中送炭	to help a lame dog over a stile
瓮中之鳖	like a rat in a hole

2. 汉语歇后语的翻译

歇后语(enigmatic folk similes)由劳动人民在日常生活中创造,具有鲜明的文化特色和浓郁的生活气息。汉语歇后语由前后两部分组成:前一部分起"引子"作用,像谜面;后一部分起"后衬"的作用,像谜底,十分自然贴切,如:八仙过海——各显神通,泥菩萨过江——自身难保,孔夫子搬家——净是书(输)等。歇后语大致分为三大类:比喻性歇后语、双关性歇后语、含有典故的歇后语。歇后语的翻译既要尽量保留源语的语言形式,又要体现源语的文化特色,因此可以采用直译、意译、套译和节译的方法。

(1) 直译

对于不包含双关语和谐音字的歇后语可以采用直译的方法,这样既保留了原歇后语的生动形象,又传播了汉语歇后语的文化内涵。

"咱们这些兵是什么兵呀,都是拿锄把子的兵,猛不乍的拿起枪来就会打仗啊?这可是瘸子担水——得一步步来么!"

(袁静等《新儿女英雄传》)

Until a few days ago, the only thing these fellows ever held in their hands was a hoe. You can't suddenly switch to a gun and expect them to know how to fight. They're <u>like cripples carrying water—you've got to lead them slowly—step by step.</u>

(沙博理 译)

正当这个工夫,一个车夫又指着他的脸说:"祥子,我说你呢,你才真是'哑巴吃扁食——心里有数儿'呢。是不是,你自己说,祥子?祥子?"

(老舍《骆驼祥子》)

Just then, another puller pointed at him and said,"I tell you, Xiangzi, <u>you're like the mute eating dumplings, you know how many you've downed!</u> Aren't you now, Xiangzi? Speak up! Hey, Xiangzi!"

(施晓菁 译)

咱们俩的事,<u>一条绳上拴着两只蚂蚱——谁也跑不了。</u>

(老舍《骆驼祥子》)

We're like two grasshoppers tied to one cord, neither can get away!

(施晓菁 译)

我看你这个人的话,真是<u>大牯牛的口水,太长</u>!

(郭沫若《屈原》)

Your words are like the slobber of a buffalo—too long!

(杨宪益 戴乃迭 译)

大鱼吃小鱼,小鱼吃虾米——弱肉强食

Big fish eat small ones and small fish swallow tiny shrimps—the weak are the prey of the strong.

千里送鹅毛——礼轻意重
To send the feather of a swan one thousand li—the gift itself may be insignificant, but the goodwill is significant.

狗拿耗子——多管闲事
A dog catching mice meddles in cat's business—to poke one's nose into other people's business.

瞎子点灯——白费蜡
A blind man lights a candle—it is useless.

老鼠过街——人人喊打
A rat runs across the street—everyone joins in the chasing and beating.

懒婆娘的裹脚布——又臭又长
The foot-bandages of a slut—long and smelly.

哑巴吃黄连——有苦说不出
Like the dumb man eating the bitter herb—He has to suffer the bitterness of it in silence.

（2）意译

含有谐音、双关或者典故的歇后语，往往可以采用意译的方法。因为谐音、典故、双关等对目的语读者来讲比较难理解，如果采用直译的话又会显得比较的冗长复杂，因此采用意译可以很好地传达歇后语的真正含义。

他这一阵心头如同<u>十五个吊桶打水，七上八下</u>，老是宁静不下来。

（周而复《上海的早晨》）

His mind was <u>in a turmoil</u> these days and he was quite unable to think straight.

（巴恩斯 译）

"十五个吊桶打水，七上八下"比喻一个人的心情非常不安，心里战战兢兢。此处译者采用了意译的方法，译出了歇后语的真正含义"in a turmoil"（心绪不宁）。

> 生活的海里起过小小的波浪，如今似乎又平静下去，一切跟平常一样，一切似乎都是外甥打灯笼，照舅（照旧）。
>
> （周立波《暴风骤雨》）
>
> The even tenor of their life had been disturbed, but things seemed to be settling down again. The villagers felt themselves back in the old rut.
>
> （许孟雄 译）

该歇后语中的"照舅"和"照旧"是谐音，没办法用英语表述出来，因此采用意译法将真正的含义翻译出来。

> "我是想：咱们是孔夫子搬家，净是书（输），心里真有点点干啥的。"
>
> （周立波《暴风骤雨》）
>
> "Only I feel bad when we lose every fight."
>
> （许孟雄 译）

孔夫子是指孔子，孔子是思想家、教育家，家里肯定有很多藏书，因此，他搬家的话，搬的东西肯定大多都是书。此处"书"与"输"的谐音，无法在英语中体现，因此采用了意译法。

> 穷棒子闹翻身，是八仙过海，各显神通。
>
> （周立波《暴风骤雨》）
>
> When we pass from the old society to the new, each of us shows his true worth.
>
> （许孟雄 译）

相传八仙过海时不用舟船，各有一套法术。民间有"八仙过海，各显神通"的谚语，比喻各自拿出本领或办法。该歇后语涉及的八仙是汉钟离、张果老、吕洞宾、铁拐李、韩湘子、曹国舅、蓝采和及何仙姑。如果全部译出来的话会非常的冗长，而且缺少文化背景的目的语读者也不能理解其真正含义，因此采用了意译法。

可是谭招弟心中却想：骑着毛驴看唱本——走着瞧吧，看究竟是啥原因。

(周而复《上海的早晨》)

But Tan Zhaodi was still thinking to herself: "Let's wait and see what the reason for it turns out to be in the end."

(巴恩斯 译)

（3）套译

部分汉语歇后语的寓意与英语的习语非常相近，此时，便可以采用套译的方法，直接借用英语中现成的习语。

怪不得人说你们"诗云子曰"的人难讲话！这样看来，你好像"老鼠尾巴上害疖子，出脓也不多！"

(吴敬梓《儒林外史》)

No wonder they say you bookworms are hard to deal with: one might just as well try to squeeze water out of a stone.

(杨宪益　戴乃迭 译)

老鼠尾巴本细小，就是生了疖子也不会太大。"老鼠尾巴上害疖子，出脓也不多"比喻才能有限，没多大的能耐。英文中有意思相近的习语，"squeeze water out of a stone"，表示设法从某物中提取出任何可能提取到的东西，但量比较小，因此此处进行了套译。

"你可倒好！肉包子打狗，一去不回头啊！"她的嗓门很高，和平日在车厂与车夫吵嘴时一样。

(老舍《骆驼祥子》)

"Well you certainly are a guy! A dog given a bone who doesn't come back for more!" Her voice was as loud as when she bawled out the rickshaw men in the yard.

(施晓菁 译)

"肉包子打狗，一去不回头"指有去无回，比喻没良心的人。这句俗语与英语中的"A dog given a bone who doesn't come back for more"非常相近，因此可以进行套译。

> **类似的例子还有很多，如：**
>
> 梅香拜把子——都是奴才
> All birds of a feather—all slaves here.
>
> 王八看绿豆——对了眼
> When Greek meets Greek.
>
> 猫哭耗子——假慈悲
> To shed crocodile tears.
>
> 山中无老虎——猴子称霸王
> When the cat's away, the mice will play.

（4）节译

当歇后语的喻义比较明显时，可以不翻译后半部分，只翻译出前半部分，保证目的语读者能够看懂即可。这种翻译方法称为节译。

> 咳！这一来，竹篮打水一场空了！
>
> （梁斌《红旗谱》）
>
> Ah! We were drawing water in a bamboo basket.
>
> （许孟雄 译）

3. 汉语谚语的翻译

谚语（proverb）指广泛流传于民间的言简意赅的短语。多数谚语反映了劳动人民的生活实践经验，而且一般是经过口头传下来的，因此多为口语形式的通俗易懂的短句或韵语。著名的哲学家弗朗西斯·培根曾说过，谚语体现了民族的智慧和精神，是人民智慧的结晶。

汉语谚语具有独特的语言特征和文化特色。从内容上来讲，谚语非常的生动，有感染力，与人类历史、日常生活及生活环境息息相关，是人们通过经历总结出来的真理，如"清明前后，种瓜点豆""种瓜得瓜，种豆得豆""独木不成林"等。从形式来看，谚语非常简短，往往以短句的形式出现，且读起来朗朗上口，如"饭后百步走,活到九十九""冬吃萝卜夏吃姜,不用医生开药方""枣芽发,种棉花"等。

汉语谚语的内容主要反映人们的社会生产生活,包括气象、农业、卫生、社会、学习等。反映气象的谚语主要来自人们长期的生活实践经验,如"朝霞不出门,晚霞行千里"。反映农业的谚语是农民在务农劳动中总结出来的经验,如"今冬麦盖三层被,来年枕着馒头睡"。反映卫生的谚语是人们根据卫生保健知识概括而成的,如"要想人长寿,多吃豆腐少吃肉"。反映社会的谚语往往是为人处事时需要注意的事项,如"人不可貌相,海水不可斗量"。反映学习的谚语一般是鼓励人们努力学习的,如"世上无难事,只怕有心人"。

基于汉语谚语的语言特点、内容特点和语用特点,汉语谚语的翻译可以采用直译、意译、套译的方法。

(1) 直译

在进行汉语谚语的英译时,为了保留源语的形象,传播中国的谚语文化,可以采用直译。

> 祥子生在北方的乡间,最忌讳随便骂街。可是他不敢打张妈,因为<u>好汉不和女斗</u>。
>
> (老舍《骆驼祥子》)
>
> Xiangzi had been brought up in a northern village where cursing was taboo. However, he dared not strike Nanny Zhang because <u>no decent man will hit a woman</u>.
>
> (施晓菁 译)

"好汉不和女斗"意思是男子汉大丈夫不和女人一般见识。此处,译者进行了直译,保留了"好汉"(decent man)和"女"(woman)。

> 孔子曰:"<u>名不正则言不顺</u>。"这原是应该极注意的。
>
> (鲁迅《阿 Q 正传》)
>
> Confucius said, "If the name is not correct, the words will not ring true"; and this axiom should be most scrupulously observed.
>
> (杨宪益 戴乃迭 译)

"名不正则言不顺"意思是名义不正当,道理就讲不通。此处直译便可使目的语读者明白该谚语的含义。

> 人往高处走,水往低处流。
> Man struggles upwards; water flows downwards.
>
> 路遥知马力,日久见人心。
> As distance tests a horse's strength, so time reveals a person's heart.

(2) 意译

有较深寓意的谚语需要进行意译,否则将无法传达谚语的内在含义,进而导致理解上的障碍。

> 吃人家嘴短,拿人家手短。
> People expect favors to be returned.
>
> （葛浩文 译）
>
> 塞翁失马,焉知非福。
> Misfortune may prove a blessing in disguise.
>
> （杨宪益 戴乃迭 译）

(3) 套译

由于谚语反映了不同的社会生活文化,而文化与语言又有一定的相通性,因此,汉语部分谚语的寓意与英语部分谚语或习语的意思相近。此时便可以采用套译法。

> 江山易改,本性难移。
> The wolf changes his coat, but not his dispositions.
>
> 一个篱笆三个桩,一个好汉三个帮。
> No flying without wings.

光打雷不下雨
All bark and no bite.

龙生龙,凤生凤,老鼠的儿子会打洞。
An onion will not produce a rose.

人不可貌相,海水不可斗量。
You can't judge a book by its cover.

练习题

一、翻译下列成语与歇后语。

1. 隔墙有耳
2. 得寸进尺
3. 石沉大海
4. 龙飞凤舞
5. 厉兵秣马
6. 木已成舟
7. 小题大做
8. 丈八的灯台——照见人家,照不见自己
9. 徐庶入曹营——一语不发
10. 隔着门缝瞧人,把人看扁啦。

二、翻译下列句子,注意加粗部分的词语,并思考如何选择合适的翻译方法。

1. 满屋里就只是他**磨牙**。
2. 祥子并没注意老头子的神气,他顾不得留神这些**闲盘儿**。
3. 等他们赶来增援时,已是"**正月十五贴门神——晚了半月啦**"。
4. **光阴似箭,稍纵即逝**。
5. 一个和尚挑水吃,两个和尚抬水吃,三个和尚没水吃。
6. 我要干这事,就**不是人**。
7. "别急!"大爷说,"**心急喝不了热粘粥**。"父亲强压住激动。

8. 爷爷说:"你**打开天窗说亮话**,要我干什么?"
9. 她说:"当家的,你把她收了吧! **肥水不流外人田**!"
10. **明枪易躲,暗箭难防**。

三、将下列段落翻译成英语。

"人之初,性本善"吗?这并非现在要加以研究的问题。但我还依稀记得,我幼小时候实未尝蓄意忤逆,对于父母,倒是极愿意孝顺的。不过年幼无知,只用了私见来解释"孝顺"的做法,以为无非是"听话""从命",以及长大之后,给年老的父母好好地吃饭罢了。

第六章 汉语委婉语的文化内涵与翻译

委婉语(Euphemism)指的是人们在人际交往中,为了避讳等而使用的好听的或者带有暗示的表达方式。在汉语文化中,很多词语及表达不能或不适合在人际交往中直截了当地说,而是要迂回曲折地运用与本意相关的话来替代。那些直接说出来会使人感到不快、不悦、不敬、羞涩或粗鲁,甚至难堪的表达方式,常被委婉语所取代(李定坤,1994)。

1. 委婉语的语言功能

汉语的委婉语从不同角度反映了人们的行为准则、社会习俗、思维模式、价值观和道德观。委婉语的语用功能主要包括回避忌讳、避免粗俗、表示礼貌等。

(1) 回避忌讳

"语言禁忌是产生委婉语的最根本的原因(张拱贵,1996)。"任何文化中都存在禁忌语(taboo),因此在交际场合需要用委婉语来表达这些禁忌语。

在汉语文化中,有许多关于"死亡"的委婉语,如薨逝、驾崩、升仙、仙逝、作古、病故、归西、圆寂等。此类委婉语在文学作品中很常见。

> 稍刻,小太监传谕出来说:"贾娘娘薨逝。" （曹雪芹《红楼梦》）
> Very soon a younger eunuch came out to announce: "The Imperial Consort Jia has passed away."
> （杨宪益　戴乃迭译）

> 若有造化,我死在老太太之先;若没造化,该讨吃的命,伏侍老太太归了西,我也不跟我老子娘哥哥去,我或是寻死,或是剪了头发当尼姑去!
> （曹雪芹《红楼梦》）
> If I'm lucky, I shall die before you, madam. Otherwise I mean to serve Your Lordship till the end of your life; then, rather than go back to my parents or to my brother, I shall commit suicide or shave my head and become a nun.
> （杨宪益　戴乃迭译）

此外,汉语中关于怀孕与生育的表达也是需要避讳的。在表达与此相关的行为时,也会使用委婉语来替代,使用"有了""有喜、身子不方便"等来表示女性怀孕,使用"诞喜""临盆""抱娃娃"等来表示女性生育。

> 方才冯紫英来看我,他见我有些抑郁之色,问我是怎么了。我才告诉他说,媳妇忽然身子有好大的不爽快,因为不得个好太医,断不透是喜是病,又不知有妨碍无妨碍。
> (曹雪芹《红楼梦》)
>
> What I was going to tell you is that Feng Ziying called just now. He asked why I looked so worried. I told him I was upset because our daughter-in-law isn't well but we can't find a good doctor to tell whether she's ill or pregnant, and whether there's any danger or not.
> (杨宪益 戴乃迭 译)

(2) 避免粗俗

在汉语文化中,若直接谈及人体器官分泌物和排泄物或者排泄行为会让人产生不愉快的感觉,有伤大雅,因此人们会使用比较含蓄或者中性的委婉语来避免粗俗,例如,大小便被称为"大解""小解""大号""小号""解手"等。

> 此时园内无人来往,只有该班的房内灯光掩映,微月半天。鸳鸯又不曾有个作伴的,也不曾提灯笼,独自一个,脚步又轻,所以该班的人皆不理会。偏生又要小解,因下了甬路,寻微草处,行至一湖山石后大桂树阴下来。
> (曹雪芹《红楼梦》)
>
> There was nobody about, and the only light apart from the faint moonlight was in the gatehouse. As she was all alone and had not brought a lantern, and as she walked quietly, no one in the gatehouse had noticed her approach. Happening just then to want to relieve herself, she left the path and walked across the grass to the back of a rockery under a large fragrant osmanthus.
> (杨宪益 戴乃迭 译)

(3) 表示礼貌

在人际交往过程中,描述他人的缺点、过失、缺陷、失败等消极事物时,需要使用委婉语,从而避免引起他人的自卑感和羞愧感,以示礼貌。

> 且说元春自选进了凤藻宫后，圣眷隆重，身体发福，未免举动费力。
>
> （曹雪芹《红楼梦》）
>
> Now, Yuanchun, highly favoured by the sagacious sovereign since her installation as Imperial Concubine in Phoenix Palace, had grown too plump to exert herself—the least fatigue made her liable to apoplexy.
>
> （杨宪益 戴乃迭 译）

2 汉语委婉语的特征

委婉语是一种社会文化现象，反映广泛的社会现象和人们的心理。为了达到"委婉"的目的，委婉语中存在比喻、借代、双关、反语等修辞现象。因此，委婉语具有含蓄性、形象性和民族性的特征。

（1）含蓄性

为了回避忌讳的事物，委婉语的表述往往采用迂回婉转的形式间接表达所描述的对象，因此具有含蓄性。

> 且今天气炎热，实不得相待，遂自行主持，命天文生择了日期入殓。寿木已系早年备下寄存在此庙的，甚是便宜。
>
> （曹雪芹《红楼梦》）
>
> As the weather was too hot for the funeral to be delayed, she decided to get an astrologer to choose a day for it. As the coffin had been prepared many years ago, and kept ever since in the temple, the funeral was easily managed.
>
> （杨宪益 戴乃迭 译）

（2）形象性

委婉语大多采用比喻、借代等修辞手法，其中的喻体往往使委婉语产生生动形象、幽默风趣的修辞效果。

> 因他自小父母替他在外娶了一个媳妇，今年二十来往年纪，生得有几分人才，见者无不羡爱。他生性轻浮，最喜拈花惹草。
>
> （曹雪芹《红楼梦》）

> While he was young his parents had found him a wife who was now just about twenty, and whose good looks were the admiration of all.
>
> But he was a flighty creature who loved nothing better than to have affairs.
>
> （杨宪益　戴乃迭 译）

拈花惹草比喻挑逗、勾引异性，到处留情。其中的"花"和"草"比喻异性。

> 鸿渐道："对呀，我呢，回国以后等于失业，教书也无所谓。辛楣出路很多，进可以做官，退可以办报，也去坐冷板凳，我替他惋惜。"
>
> （钱钟书《围城》）
>
> Hung-chien said, "That's right. Coming back home has meant unemployment, so I don't mind teaching. But Hsin-mei has several options open to him. He can either work for the government or run a newspaper, but instead he's going to sit on a cold bench. I feel sorry for him."
>
> （珍妮·凯利　毛国权 译）

（3）民族性

由于民族文化的差异，不同民族在生活习俗、思维模式、宗教信仰等方面存在较大的差异。文化的差异一定程度地体现在语言上，委婉语作为语言文化的一部分，也传递了不同民族的文化特征，因此，具有一定的民族性。

> 忽见东府里几个人慌慌张张跑来说："老爷殡天了！"众人听了，唬了一大跳，忙都说："好好的并无疾病，怎么就没了！"下人说："老爷天天修炼，定是功成圆满，升仙去了。"
>
> （曹雪芹《红楼梦》）
>
> Some servants from the Eastern Mansion came rushing up frantically. "The old master's ascended to Heaven!" They announced. Everybody was consternated. "He wasn't even ill, how could he pass away so suddenly?" They exclaimed. The servants explained, "His Lordship took elixirs every day; now he must have achieved his aim and become an immortal."
>
> （杨宪益　戴乃迭 译）

3　汉语委婉语的翻译

由于委婉语具有特定的语义功能和特征,且体现了不同的思维方式、审美标准和价值观念,因此,汉语委婉语的翻译应依据语境选择直译或意译。

（1）直译

为了保留汉语委婉语的文化特征,通常采用直译的方法,这样可以保持源语的神韵风格,体现源语的情感与含蓄性。如:

> 三月里刘熏宇君来信,说互生病了,而且是没有希望的病,医生说只好<u>等日子</u>了。四月底在《时事新报》上见到立达学校的通告,想不到这么快互生就殁了! 后来听说他病中的光景,那实在太惨;为他想,早点去,少吃些苦头,也未尝不好的。但丢下立达这个学校,这班朋友,这班学生,他一定不甘心,不<u>瞑目</u>!
>
> （朱自清《哀互生》）
>
> In March I heard from Mr. Liu Xunyu that Husheng was sick and hopeless sick at that. The doctor said there was nothing he could do but to <u>wait for the day to arrive</u>. Toward the end of April, I came across an obituary issued by Lida School in the newspaper *Current Affairs*. How quickly the day had arrived! Later, when I learned how he had suffered during his illness, I thought it was too miserable. From his point of view, however, his passing away was not a bad thing after all, because he suffered less by going earlier. But it must have been very hard for him to <u>close his eyes</u> and resign himself to the fact that he was leaving his Lida School, his friends and his students behind!
>
> （刘士聪 译）

"等日子"指的是等待死去的那一天,"瞑目"是指闭上眼睛,多指人死时无所牵挂。此处将二者分别直译为"wait for the day to arrive"和"close his eyes",很好地保留了汉语委婉语的含蓄性。

> 赵姨娘道:"我不是鸳鸯,她早到仙界去了。"
>
> (曹雪芹《红楼梦》)
>
> "I'm not Yuan-yang," protested Concubine Zhao, "She's long since gone to the immortal's realm."
>
> (杨宪益 戴乃迭 译)

"到仙界去了"指人死了,是人们对于死亡的一种含蓄的表述方式。该委婉语的直译保留了其民族性。

> 凤姐儿未等王夫人开口,先说道:"老太太昨日还说要来着呢,因为晚上看见宝兄弟他们吃桃儿,老人家又嘴馋,吃了有大半个,五更天的时候就一连起来了两次,今日早餐略觉身子倦些。"
>
> (曹雪芹《红楼梦》)
>
> "Up to yesterday she meant to come," explained Xifeng before Lady Wang could get a word in. "But yesterday evening she saw Baoyu eating some peaches and she couldn't resist eating nearly a whole peach. She had to get up twice just before dawn, which left her tired out this morning."
>
> (杨宪益 戴乃迭 译)

在这个语境"起来"中指贾母因桃子吃多了而导致晚上腹泻,因此晚上起来上厕所。此处,为了避免粗俗,用"起来"表示拉肚子上厕所。该委婉语的直译显现了源语的含蓄性。

> 老祖宗看看,谁不是你老人家的儿女?难道将来只有宝兄弟顶你老人家上五台山不成?那些东西只留给他!
>
> (曹雪芹《红楼梦》)
>
> Look, aren't all of us your children? Is Baoyu the only one who'll carry you as an immortal on his head to Mount Wutai, that you keep everything for him?
>
> (杨宪益 戴乃迭 译)

"五台山"是佛教圣地,把信徒抬上五台山即说明他已离世了。此处,译者采用直译,保留了原文的民族性特征。

(2) 意译

> 今只有嫡妻贾氏,生得一女,乳名黛玉,年方五岁。夫妻无子,故爱如珍宝,且又见他聪明清秀,便也欲使他读书识得几个字,不过假充养子之意,聊解<u>膝下荒凉</u>之叹。
>
> (曹雪芹《红楼梦》)
>
> By his wife, nee Jia, he had a daughter Daiyu just five years old. Both parents loved her dearly. And because she was as intelligent as she was pretty, they decided to give a good education to make up for <u>their lack of a son</u> and help them forget their loss.
>
> (杨宪益 戴乃迭 译)

"膝下荒凉"是无子女或子女少的委婉说法。此处译者进行了意译,能更好地传达其内在含义。

> "合家大小,远近亲友,谁不知我这媳妇比儿子还强十倍。如今<u>伸腿去了</u>,可见这长房内绝灭无人了。"说着又哭起来。
>
> "Everyone in the family, old and young, distant kin or close friends, knows that my daughter-in-law was infinitely superior to my son. Now that <u>she has gone</u>, my branch of the family is fated to die out." With that he broke down again.

"伸腿去了"指人死去了,如果进行直译,有可能会导致目的语读者的误解,因此译者采用了意译。

> 大夫便说:"替夫人奶奶们道喜,姐儿发热是<u>见喜</u>了,并非别病。"
>
> (曹雪芹《红楼梦》)
>
> "I am happy to inform Her Ladyship and Madam Lien that the little girl's fever is simply due to <u>smallpox</u>."
>
> (杨宪益 戴乃迭 译)

"见喜"指小儿痘疹(天花),旧时这个病为险症,人们忌讳直说,又因为出过天花后可望平安,所以称为"见喜"。如果将字面意思译为英语,英语读者仅仅从言语形式不能推测出信息的实指内容,因此译者采用了意译。

> 偏偏今日早晨他兄弟来瞧他，谁知那小孩子家不知好歹，看见他姐姐身上不爽快，就有事也不当告诉他，别说是这么一点子小事。
>
> （曹雪芹《红楼梦》）
>
> But then her brother had to come and see her this morning. He's too young to know any better, but when he saw she was ill he shouldn't have troubled her with his affairs, not to say a trifle like this.
>
> （杨宪益　戴乃迭 译）

"身上不爽快"指身体不舒服，如果直译会让目的语读者产生误解，因此译者采用了意译，将其译为 ill。

练习题

一、将下列句子翻译成英语，注意其中委婉语的翻译方法。

1. 不错，然而这位老太爷就快要断气了。
2. 根据她的经验，她明白了，这准是去会相好的呀！
3. 聂耳在 23 岁的青春年华中过早地写下了他生命的休止符。
4. 为了我们的事业，我已将生死置之度外，如有不幸，就把我埋在阴山顶上。
5. 南院马棚里走了水，不相干，已经救下去了。
6. 鸳鸯只当她和别的女孩子也在此方便。
7. 且说宝玉次日起来，梳洗完毕，早有小厮们传话进来说："老爷叫二爷说话。"
8. 袭人之母业已停床，不能回来。
9. 平儿愈听愈惨，想来实在难处，恐凤姐自寻短见，只得紧紧守着。

第七章 汉语颜色词的文化内涵与翻译

柏拉图和亚里士多德这两位先哲很早就开始了关于颜色及颜色感知的研究。柏拉图提出人类感知颜色的三项基本条件:光源、反光物体、能接受反光功能的眼睛。颜色是人们对于客观世界的一种感知。颜色词是人们形容颜色的词汇和词语。不同民族、不同文化背景促生了不同的颜色文化。生活在不同文化中的人对颜色有不同的解读,颜色对不同民族的人也有不同的意义。在不同的民族文化中,同样的颜色可能表达不同的文化心理和文化内涵。

1. 汉语颜色词的分类

汉语的颜色词有大概两千多个,可分为三大类:基本颜色词、实物颜色词和色差颜色词(包惠南,2004)。

基本颜色词是那些本来就用来表达实物颜色的词汇,如:赤(red)、橙(orange)、黄(yellow)、绿(green)、青(indigo)、蓝(blue)、紫(violet)、黑(black)、灰(gray)、褐(brown)等。

> 鸳鸯穿着水红绫子袄儿,青缎子背心,束着白绉绸汗巾儿。
>
> (曹雪芹《红楼梦》)
>
> Yuanyang was wearing a pink silk jacket, a sleeveless black satin jacket and a white silk sash.
>
> (杨宪益 戴乃迭 译)

实物颜色词就是用自然界中物体的本色来表示颜色的词汇。汉语中存在大量的实物颜色词。实物颜色词能够更生动、更形象地描绘事物的颜色。相较于基本颜色词的概括性意义,实物颜色词能够表示颜色的不同程度,如"深、浅、淡、暗"等。汉语中的实物颜色词多与各民族赖以生存的自然环境有关。

(1)与植物相关的实物颜色词

汉语文化中有许多与植物相关的颜色,如:桃红(pink)、杏红(apricot pink)、梅红色(plum)、枣红色(claret)、橙黄(orange)、藤黄(rattan yellow)、杏黄(apricot yellow)、橄榄绿(olive green)、苹果绿(apple green)、花白(grey)、茶色(dark brown)、玫瑰紫(rose violet)、海棠红(cerise)、葱绿(light green)、豆青(pea green)、橘红(orange red)。

> 那芳官只穿着海棠红的小棉袄……
>
> （曹雪芹《红楼梦》）
>
> Meanwhile Fangguan, wearing only a cerise padded jacket…
>
> （杨宪益 戴乃迭 译）

> 宝玉道:"松花色配什么?"莺儿道:"松花配桃红。"宝玉道:"也罢了。也打一条桃红,再打一条葱绿。"
>
> （曹雪芹《红楼梦》）
>
> "What would match a light green one?" asked Bao-yu.
> "That would go well with peach-pink."
> "All right. Do me one also in peach-pink and another in leek-green."
>
> （杨宪益 戴乃迭 译）

> 每人一个奶娘并一个丫头照管,余者在外面上夜听唤。一面早有熙凤命人送了一顶藕合色花帐,并几件锦被缎褥之类。
>
> （曹雪芹《红楼梦》）
>
> Each would be attended by a nurse and a maid, while other attendants were on night duties outside. Xifeng had already sent round a flowered lavender curtain, satin quilts and embroidered mattresses.
>
> （杨宪益 戴乃迭 译）

(2) 与动物相关的实物颜色词

汉语文化中有许多与动物相关的颜色词,非常形象、直观,如:驼色(camel)、鹅黄(light yellow)、蟹青(greenish-grey)、孔雀蓝(peacock blue)、象牙白(ivory)等。

(3) 与珠宝和矿物相关的实物颜色词

生活中有许多颜色词不是单一的颜色,而是复合颜色。自然界中的珠宝及矿物颜色比较丰富,因此,汉语中有许多与珠宝和矿物有关的颜色词汇,如:银白

(silver)、金色(golden)、玛瑙红(agate red)、古铜色(bronze)、翠绿(emerald green)等。

> 身上穿着银红撒花半旧大袄……
> （曹雪芹《红楼梦》）
> …his coat of a flower pattern on a bright red ground was not new…
> （杨宪益　戴乃迭 译）

（4）与自然现象相关的实物颜色词

为了形象地表述具体的颜色，汉语中有很多与自然现象相关的颜色词汇，如：雪白(snow white)、火红(flaming)、天蓝(azure)等。

> 她穿着半新的藕合色……下面水绿裙子。
> （曹雪芹《红楼梦》）
> The maid was wearing a light purple silk tunic…and a pale green skirt.
> （杨宪益　戴乃迭 译）

在阳光的照射下，各种颜色会显现不同的颜色，深浅明暗有别。汉语中常用色差颜色词来表现颜色的不同，如：深蓝(dark blue)、蔚蓝(azure)、鲜红(bright red)、暗红(dark red)、嫩绿(light green)、漆黑(pitch-black)、淡灰(light gray)、浅黄(light yellow)等。

> 他懒得去拿那冰凉的车把，怕那噎得使人恶心的风。狂风怕日落，直到四点多钟，风才完全静止，昏黄的天上透出些夕照的微红。
> （老舍《骆驼祥子》）
> He didn't feel like holding those icy cold shafts and was afraid of that choking, sickening blast. By four in the afternoon the sun went down, and the wind dropped completely, while some evening pink appeared in the dusty sky.
> （施晓菁 译）

> 御河的水久已冻好，静静的，灰亮的，坦平的，坚固的，拖着那禁城的城墙。
> （老舍《骆驼祥子》）
> The moat, long since frozen over, stretched silent, silver-grey, flat and solid around the walls of the Forbidden City.
> （施晓菁 译）

2. 汉语颜色词的文化内涵

不同民族的文化决定了人们对同种颜色内涵的解读不同。颜色的文化内涵由语言因素、社会因素、认知因素及思维方式等共同决定。中华民族的文化传统与颜色息息相关。

(1) 黑色的文化内涵

在古代的中国,黑色是北方的象征,代表"水",五色之一。黑色在《易经》中被认为是"天"的颜色,是众母之色。"天地玄黄"之说,源于古人感觉到北方天空长时期都显现出神秘的黑色。他们认为,北极星是天帝的位置。黑色在古代的中国,为众色之长。新石器时期的黑陶可以说明中国人尚黑。《韩非子·十过篇》中记载:"尧禅天在,虞舜受之。作为食器,斩山木而材之,削锯修之迹,流漆墨其上:输之于宫,为食器……舜禅天下而传之于禹,禹作祭器,墨染其外,朱画其内。"尧、舜、禹时代的先民也崇尚黑色。公元前221年,秦始皇统一中国时,就依据先人观物取象的传统,最终定黑色为尊,"以冬10月为年首,色上黑。"秦始皇即位之后,"易服色与旗色为黑"(余雯蔚 & 周武忠,2007)。

以老庄为代表的道家也崇尚玄色(黑色),认为"五色令人目盲,五音令人耳聋",只有最简单朴素的黑色最能表现"道"。在戏曲文化中,黑色代表刚正无私,如宋代的包拯就为黑面。

黑色作为颜色最深的颜色,具有多种不同的文化意义,而不同的文化意义又经由语言表现在词汇上。

黑色可以代表黑暗与神秘,如"黑灯瞎火"(dark)、"黑不溜秋"(swarthy)、"黑影"(shadow)、"黑洞"(black hole)等;黑色可以表示隐秘、罪恶、不合法,例如形容人心肠阴险狠毒就可以说"黑心"(evil mind),非法地下秩序的有组织犯罪团伙叫"黑社会"(gangsterdom),代别人受过叫"背黑锅"(bear the blame),不法交易市场叫"黑市"(black market),用卑劣的隐性手段谋取利益叫"黑幕"(inside story of a plot),实施犯罪行动而组成的邪派组织叫"黑道"(underworld),不正当的手段称为"黑手"(evil backstage manipulator),非法所得的钱叫作"黑钱"(illegal income),还有"黑名单"(blacklist)、"黑客"(hacker)等。

再说,这个事要是吵嚷开,被刘四知道了呢?刘四晓得不晓得他女儿是个破货呢?假若不知道,祥子岂不独自背上黑锅?

(老舍《骆驼祥子》)

What's more, what if word of this spread and reached Fourth Master Liu's ears? Did he know that his daughter was a tart? If he didn't, then wouldn't he put the whole blame on Xiangzi?

(包惠南 译)

(2) 白色的文化内涵

白色在汉语文化中有多种含义,大体上分为褒义和贬义两大类。

白色可以表示纯洁(purity),代表清流贤正,如:

粉身碎骨浑不怕,要留清白在人间。

(于谦《石灰吟》)

Though broken into pieces, you will have no fright;
You'll purify the world by washing it e'er white.

(许渊冲 译)

白色可以表示明亮(brightness),与暗相对,引申义为明白、清楚,如真相大白(the truth has been brought into daylight)、明明白白(as clear as noonday)、一清二白(spotless)等。

白色可以表示观点或行动极端保守或反动。中国的革命文化称为红色文化,与其相对的反动的、反革命的即为白色,如白匪、白色政权、白色恐怖、白贼、白狗子等。

红妹妹问我:"你找到了游击队,还回来吗?"

我说:"不回来了。"但我觉得这话说得不周全,又说:"等到打完国民党、白狗子,我再回来。"

"Are you coming back after you've found the guerrilla?" She asked.

"No," I replied. "That is," I hastened to add, "not until we've wiped out the Kuomintang reactionaries and their White guards."

(卢红梅 2006:184)

白色可以表示没有效果、徒然，如白干、白费力气、一穷二白、白搭等。

> 等本钱都吃进去，再去拉车，还不是脱了裤子放屁，白白赔上五块钱？
>
> （老舍《骆驼祥子》）
>
> If he sank his capital in this only to end up pulling a rickshaw again, it would be like stripping off his pants to fart——a complete waste of five dollars.
>
> （施晓菁 译）

白色是古代丧服的颜色，因此也作丧事的代称，象征凶事。中国古代五方说中，西方为白虎，白虎是刑天杀神，主萧杀三秋，因此白色是无血色、无生命的象征，寓示死亡或凶兆。自古以来，有亲人死亡，其家属要穿白色丧服，设白色灵堂，出殡时要打白纸幡，撒白纸钱。民间称婚丧大事为"红白事"，"白事"就是指丧事。因此中国传统文化中，白色通常与恐惧和悲哀联系在一起，逐渐成了传统文化中忌讳的颜色（祖林，2011）。

> 明儿又要送南安府里的礼，又要预备娘娘的重阳节礼，还有几家红白大礼。
>
> （曹雪芹《红楼梦》）
>
> Tomorrow I have to send presents to the Prince of Nan'an and prepare Double-Ninth gifts for Her Imperial Highness; then there are weddings and funerals coming up in several other families too.
>
> （杨宪益　戴乃迭 译）

白色还象征卑贱与贫寒。诗句"谈笑有鸿儒，往来无白丁"中的"白丁"在中国封建社会里指没文化、没功名的人。平民穿的衣服称白衣，白身指没有官职或功名的人，他们住的茅屋叫白屋（祖林，2011）。

> 贾敬虽白衣无功于国，念彼祖父之功，追赐五品之职。
>
> （曹雪芹《红楼梦》）
>
> Though Jia Jing was an ordinary citizen who performed no special service for the state, in view of his grand-father's merit he is to be promoted posthumously to the fifth rank.
>
> （杨宪益　戴乃迭 译）

・红色的文化内涵

红是表示红色的基本颜色词,在中国文化中,红色又细分为绛红、大红、朱红、嫣红、深红、水红、橘红、杏红等。红色作为人们广泛使用的颜色,在汉语文化中有着不同的文化内涵。

在中国传统文化中,红色象征着喜庆、欢乐。春节期间,家家都要贴红色春联、挂红灯笼、贴红福字。中国人喜爱红,认为红是吉祥的象征,所以传统婚礼习俗总以大红色烘托喜庆、热烈的气氛。在中国的传统婚礼上,新娘要着红装,盖红盖头,婚房也要用红布装饰。因此,红色在我国也被称作中国红。

按照传统,皇帝和皇后新婚第一夜,要在坤宁宫里一间不过十米见方的喜房里度过。这间屋子的特色是:没有什么陈设,炕占去了四分之一,除了地皮,全涂上了红色。行过"合卺礼",吃过了"子孙饽饽",进入这间一片暗红色的屋子里,我觉得很憋气。新娘子坐在炕上,低着头,我在旁边看了一会儿,只觉着眼前一片红:红帐子、红褥子、红衣、红裙、红花朵、红脸蛋……好像一摊溶化了的红蜡烛。

(溥仪《我的前半生》)

According to tradition the emperor and the empress spent their wedding night in a bridal chamber some ten metres square in the Palace of Earthly Peace (Kun Ning Gong). This was a rather peculiar room—it was unfurnished except for the bed-platform which filled a quarter of it, and everything about it except the floor was red. When we had drunk the nuptial cup and eaten sons-and-grandsons cakes and entered this dark red room I felt stifled. The bride sat on the bed, her head bent down. I looked around me and saw that everything was red—red bed-curtains, red pillows, a red dress, a red skirt, red flowers, and a red face… it all looked like a melted red wax candle.

(包惠南 译)

可巧连日有王公侯伯世袭官员十几处,皆系荣宁非亲即友或世交之家,或有升迁,或有黜降,或有婚嫁红白等事,王夫人贺吊迎送,应酬不暇,前边更无人。

(曹雪芹《红楼梦》)

It happened now that a dozen or so promotions, demotions, marriages or funerals in the families of nobles or hereditary officials related to or friendly with the Rong and Ning houses kept Lady Wang busy for several days in a row, paying visits of congratulation or condolence. This left her less time than ever to attend to affairs at home.

(杨宪益 戴乃迭 译)

红色象征着顺利与成功,如日常生活中我们常说红人、走红、爆红、红榜、开门红、满堂红等。红色也象征权贵,古代的达官贵人喜用红色装饰门庭,唐代诗人杜甫的《自京赴奉先咏怀五百字》提到"朱门酒肉臭,路有冻死骨",这里的"朱"即红色,意思是贵族人家的红漆大门里散发出酒肉的香味,穷人们却在街头因冻饿而死。

如君坊的酒比别的酒家贵,可生意却越来越红火,这可忙坏了文君和相如。

(徐飞《凤求凰》)

In spite of the high price of its wine, the Rujun Tavern was doing a roaring trade. Wenjun and Xiangru were run off their feet.

(保罗·怀特)

在中国,红色的政治色彩浓厚,是社会主义、革命文化及无产阶级的象征。我们的革命文化被称作红色文化,革命景点称为红色景点,革命精神称为红色精神,革命政权称为红色政权,革命根据地称为红区,革命歌曲称为红歌,与此相关的其他词汇还有红卫兵、红领巾等。

"静,想不到你变化得这么快……"沉了半晌才接着说,"我,我要求你别这样……这是危险的!一顶红帽子往你头上一戴,要杀头的呀!"

(杨沫《青春之歌》)

"Daojing, I can hardly believe you've changed so quickly…" After a moment's silence he continued, "I implore you not to go on like this—it's too dangerous. Once you're branded as a Red, they can cut off your head!"

(包惠南 译)

此外,红色还象征危险,例如"红灯"起警示作用。在戏曲文化中,红色象征着正义,勾画红色脸谱的演员通常扮演正面角色,如关羽、赵匡胤、姜维等。

(4) 黄色的文化内涵

黄色是温暖的颜色,给人愉快、辉煌、温暖的感觉。黄色在中国文化中有多种内在含义。

黄色在汉语文化中曾是皇室的象征。古代崇尚黄色,因为黄色常常被看作君权的象征。在中国的阴阳学说中,黄色对应五行中的土,这种土是在宇宙中央的"中央土",在五行当中,土为尊。此后这种思想又与儒家大一统思想糅合在一起,认为统一的王朝就是这样一个处于"中央土"的帝国,有别于周边的四夷。这样,黄色就与正统、尊崇联系起来,为君主的统治提供了合理性的论证。再加上古代又有"龙战于野,其血玄黄"的说法,而君主又以龙为象征,因此黄色与君主就产生了更为直接的联系。

> 宝钗亦悄悄的笑道:"还不快作上去,只管姐姐妹妹的。谁是你姐姐?那上头穿<u>黄袍</u>的才是你姐姐,你又认我这姐姐来了。"
>
> (曹雪芹《红楼梦》)
>
> Suppressing a smile Baochai replied, "Hurry up and finish instead of talking such nonsense. Who are you calling 'sister'? That's your sister sitting up there in the <u>golden robes</u>. Why call me your sister?"
>
> (杨宪益 戴乃迭 译)

黄色是金子的颜色,因此,日常生活中我们会用黄色来象征财富和宝贵。例如,黄金屋形容极其富贵奢华的生活环境;黄金时代指政治、经济、文化的昌盛时期,也指人一生中最宝贵的时期;黄金时段指一天中用户数量非常集中的一个或几个时间段;黄金地段指城市中交通便利、商业繁华的地方等。

此外,黄色还象征着死亡,如"黄泉"(the world of the dead)。黄色还可以表示不成功,如买卖黄了。

3. 汉语颜色词的翻译

在颜色词的翻译过程中,汉语中的很多颜色词在英语中有对应的颜色词,此时采用直译既可以准确传达原文意思,又保持了汉语的颜色词汇所带有的文化

特色。如:

> 色味当五藏:白当肺、辛。
>
> 《黄帝内经·素问》
>
> The five colors and the five tastes correspond to the five zang organs. So we can say that the white color and pungent taste correspond to the lungs.
>
> (倪毛信 译)

原文的意思是"色、味与五脏"相应:白色和辛味应于肺。肺对应白色因此这里将白色直译为"white"。

> 台矶之上,坐着几个穿红着绿的丫鬟,一见他们来了,便忙都笑迎上来,……
>
> (曹雪芹《红楼梦》)
>
> Several maids dressed in red and green rose from the terrace and hurried to greet them with smiles.
>
> (杨宪益 戴乃迭 译)

在汉语文化中,有些颜色词所指的颜色并不是字面义,此时需要进行替换翻译,以表达出其真正所指。如:

> 太阳之脉,其终也,戴眼,反折瘛疭,其色白,绝汗乃出,出则死矣。
>
> 《黄帝内经·素问》
>
> When the taiyang/bladder and small intestine channel collapses, the patient will manifest opisthotonos, a stiffness of the back, convulsive spasms, paleness, and spontaneous sweating.
>
> (倪毛信 译)

原文的意思是"太阳经脉气绝的时候,病人两目上视,身背反张,手足抽掣,面色发白,出绝汗,绝汗一出,便要死亡了。""其色白"指的是面色发白,为经脉气绝的面色惨白,因此不能直译为 white,而应译为 paleness。

> 他(祥子)很想换一份套子,换上<u>土黄</u>或<u>月白色儿</u>的,或者足以减去一点素净劲儿。
>
> (老舍《骆驼祥子》)
>
> He felt like changing the metal work to something <u>bronze</u> or <u>milky in color</u>, to liven it up a bit.
>
> (施晓菁 译)
>
> 但见黛玉身上穿着<u>月白</u>绣花小毛皮袄,加上银鼠坎肩;头上挽着随常云髻,簪上一枝赤金匾簪,别无花朵,腰下系着<u>杨妃色</u>绣花绵裙。
>
> (曹雪芹《红楼梦》)
>
> He noticed now that Daiyu was wearing a <u>pale-blue</u> embroidered fur-lined jacket under a short white squirrel tunic, and a <u>pink</u> embroidered silk padded skirt of the kind worn by Lady Yang.
>
> (杨宪益 戴乃迭 译)

月白指的是淡蓝色,因近似月色,故称月白,其实指的就是月亮的颜色。古人认为月亮的颜色并不是纯白,而是带着一点淡淡的蓝色。杨妃色中的"妃"古同"绯",因此,杨妃色即粉红色。该例子中的两个颜色词均不能进行直译,因此译者对其进行了意译,分别译为 pale-blue 和 pink。

由于中西方文化的差异,一些具有引申意义的颜色词往往不能进行直译,而需根据不同的文化习俗和价值观对其进行意译,从而准确传达颜色词的内在含义。如:

> 老头子……仿佛看到了自己死了的时候也不过就是这样,不过是把喜棚改作<u>白棚</u>而已,棺材前边没有儿孙们穿孝跪灵,只有些不相干的人们打麻将守夜!
>
> (老舍《骆驼祥子》)
>
> At his death it would be just like this, he thought, only <u>the marquee</u> of felicity would be changed into one of <u>mourning</u>; but there would be no sons or grandsons to wear mourning clothes and kneel in vigil before his coffin, only some casual acquaintances who would play mahjong during the night watch.
>
> (包惠南 译)

白棚指的是办丧事的地方,此处译者对其进行了意译,译为 the marquee of mourning。

练习题

一、将下列句子翻译成英语,注意其中颜色词的翻译。

1. 一色水磨群墙,下面白石台矶,凿成西番草花样。

2. 忽抬头看见前面一带粉垣,里面数楹修舍,有千百竿翠竹遮掩。

3. 那些奇草仙藤愈冷愈苍翠,都结了实,似珊瑚豆子一般,累垂可爱。

4. 那廊下金架子上站的绿毛红嘴是鹦哥儿,我是认得的。那笼子里黑老鸹子怎么又长出凤头来,也会说话呢。

5. 一径引人绕着碧桃花,穿过一层竹篱花障编就的月洞门,俄见粉墙环护,绿柳周垂。

6. 那一边乃是一棵西府海棠,其势若伞,丝垂翠缕,葩吐丹砂。

7. 粉面含春威不露,丹唇未启笑先闻。

8. 即使他今天买上明天就丢了,他也得去买。这是他的志愿、希望,甚至是信仰。不拉着自己的车,他简直像是白活。

9. 从此以后,陈皇后每日只能以泪洗面,长门宫那扇朱漆大门,她是无论如何也出不去了。

10. 1933年夏天,北平党组织遭受到严重的破坏,剩下来的少数同志,在残酷的白色恐怖中,风雨飘摇,随时都处在被捕的危险中。

二、将下列段落翻译成英语,注意其中颜色词的翻译。

灰天上透出些红色,地与远树显着更黑了;红色渐渐的与灰色融调起来,有的地方成为灰紫的,有的地方特别的红,而大部分的天色是葡萄灰的。又待了一会儿,红中透出明亮的金黄来,各种颜色都露出些光;忽然,一切东西都非常的清楚了。跟着,东方的早霞变成一片深红,头上的天显出蓝色。红霞碎开,金光一道一道的射出,横的是霞,直的是光,在下的东南织成一部极伟大光华的蛛网:绿的田,树,野草,都由暗绿变为发光的翡翠。老松的干上染上了金红,飞鸟的翅儿闪起金光,一切的东西都带出笑意。

实践篇

PRACTICE

翻译实训

1. 新时代的中国青年

  青年是整个社会力量中最积极、最有生气的力量,国家的希望在青年,民族的未来在青年。①中国青年始终是实现中华民族伟大复兴的先锋力量。

  近代以后,中国逐步沦为半殖民地半封建社会,国家蒙辱、人民蒙难、文明蒙尘,中华民族遭受了前所未有的劫难,中国青年深切感受到日益深重的民族危机。②

  中国青年的觉醒,点燃了中华民族伟大复兴的希望之光。五四运动前后,一大批率先接受新思想、新文化、新知识的有志青年在反复比较中选择了马克思列宁主义,促进中国人民和中华民族实现了自鸦片战争以来的第一次全面觉醒。③1921年7月,平均年龄仅28岁的13位代表参加了中国共产党第一次全国代表大会,宣告了中国共产党诞生这一开天辟地的大事件,吹响了全民族觉醒和奋起的号角,开启了民族复兴的新纪元。④在中国共产党的领导下,中国共产主义青年团于1922年成立,中国青年运动翻开了新的历史篇章。

  回首百年,无论风云变幻、沧海桑田,中国青年爱党、爱国、爱人民的赤诚追求始终未改,坚定不移听党话、跟党走的忠贞初心始终未变。⑤在新民主主义革命时期,中国青年不怕牺牲、敢于斗争,经受了生与死的考验,为争取民族独立、人民解放,冲锋陷阵、抛洒热血。⑥在社会主义革命和建设时期,中国青年勇于拼搏、甘于奉献,经受了苦与乐的考验,在新中国的广阔天地忘我劳动、发愤图强。⑦在改革开放和社会主义现代化建设新时期,中国青年开拓创新、勇立潮头,经受了得与失的考验,为推动中国大踏步赶上时代锐意改革、拼搏奋进。⑧

  党的十八大以来,中国特色社会主义进入新时代。⑨以习近平同志为核心的党中央高度重视青年、热情关怀青年、充分信任青年,明确提出党管青年原则,大力倡导青年优先发展理念,着力发挥共青团作为党的助手和后备军作用,推动青年发展事业,实现全方位进步,取得历史性成就。⑩在这个伟大的新时代,中国青年展现了亮丽的青春风采、迸发出豪迈的青春激情。⑪

新时代中国青年刚健自信、胸怀天下、担当有为,衷心拥护党的领导,奋力走在时代前列,展现出前所未有的昂扬风貌:追求远大理想,心中铭刻着对马克思主义的崇高信仰、对共产主义和中国特色社会主义的坚定信念;深植家国情怀,与国家同呼吸、与人民共命运,时刻彰显着鲜明的爱国主义精神气质;传承奋斗担当,先天下之忧而忧、后天下之乐而乐,勇做走在时代前列的奋进者、开拓者、奉献者。⑫

历史清晰而深刻地昭示,没有中国共产党就没有朝气蓬勃的中国青年运动,矢志不渝跟党走是中国青年百年奋斗的最宝贵经验,深深融入血脉的红色基因是中国青年百年奋斗的最宝贵财富。⑬

2021年7月1日,习近平总书记在庆祝中国共产党成立100周年大会上深情寄语:"新时代的中国青年要以实现中华民族伟大复兴为己任,增强做中国人的志气、骨气、底气,不负时代,不负韶华,不负党和人民的殷切期望!"⑭

展望未来,民族复兴大业已经站在新的历史起点、踏上新的伟大征程。新时代中国青年迎来了实现抱负、施展才华的难得机遇,更肩负着建设社会主义现代化强国、实现中华民族伟大复兴中国梦的时代重任。

中国梦是历史的、现实的,也是未来的;是广大人民的,更是青年一代的。新时代中国青年必将以永不懈怠的精神状态、永不停滞的前进姿态,在接续奋斗中将中华民族伟大复兴的中国梦变为现实。⑮(中国日报网,2022)

词汇:

民族复兴 national rejuvenation

半殖民地半封建社会 a semi-colonial, semi-feudal society

民族危机 national crisis

五四运动 the May Fourth Movement in 1919

马克思列宁主义 Marxism-Leninism

鸦片战争 the Opium War

中国共产党第一次全国代表大会 the First National Congress of the Communist Party of China(CPC)

中国共产主义青年团 the Communist Youth League of China(CYLC)

新民主主义革命 the New Democratic Revolution(1919—1949)

社会主义革命和建设 the socialist revolution and reconstruction

党的十八大 the 18th CPC National Congress

党中央 the CPC Central Committee

翻译解析：

1. 该句由三个小句构成，语义信息可分为两个部分，第一个小句重点说明青年是什么，第二、三小句介绍青年的重要价值，他们肩负着"国家的希望"与"民族的未来"。鉴于源语的叙述层次及英语的行文便利，将该句拆分为两个句子进行翻译。

2. 该句由五部分构成，如果将其翻译为一个英语句子，不利于英语的行文表达，因此根据叙述层次将其拆分为三个句子来译。"近代以后"翻译为"After 1840"，时间概念更加明确，有利于提升英文表达的准确性及读者的理解。从叙述逻辑而言，"中华民族遭受了前所未有的劫难"统领"国家蒙辱、人民蒙难、文明蒙尘"，因此可将"中华民族遭受了前所未有的劫难"置于"国家蒙辱、人民蒙难、文明蒙尘"之前翻译；该短句与"中国逐步沦为半殖民地半封建社会"形成并列关系，因此在译文中两句用并列连词 and 进行衔接，以增强译文的逻辑性，符合英语的行文习惯。

3. 该句由三个部分构成，译文在处理第一部分"五四运动前后"时添加了具体的时间概念，将其翻译为"Around the May Fourth Movement in 1919"，有利于不了解中国近代史的英文读者准确定位时间。第二部分语言信息较多，尤其是主语"一大批率先接受新思想、新文化、新知识的有志青年"。该主语的核心词为"青年"，根据该词的实指概念及当时的社会背景，译文将其翻译为"aspiring and progressive young intellectuals"，并将该主语转化为独立的句子进行翻译，谓语为"assumed the lead in"，既保留了源语逻辑思维的完整性，又增强了译文的可读性。第三部分"促进中国人民和中华民族实现了自鸦片战争以来的第一次全面觉醒"是中国青年选择马克思列宁主义的结果。根据叙述逻辑，译文将其作为第二部分中的"有志青年在反复比较中选择了马克思列宁主义"的非限定性定语从句进行翻译，用"led to"表示结果，语言逻辑清晰，语义内容完整。

4. 该句由五部分构成，各部分之间无任何表明逻辑关系的衔接词，凸显了汉语重意合的特点。首先，译文根据叙述逻辑，将"13位代表"作为主语进行翻译，谓语动词为"参加"及"宣告"，并用 and 进行并列衔接，符合源语的逻辑层次及英语重形合的特点。其次，译文根据源语叙述逻辑，将"这一开天辟地的大事件"作为"中国共产党诞生"的同位语进行翻译,"吹响了全民族觉醒和奋起的号角"作为定语从句来修饰限定该同位语。最后,将"开启了民族复兴的新纪元"独立成句,既有利于突出该语言信息,又有利于英语的行文便利,增强了译文的可读性。

5. 该句由四部分构成,第二部分中的"风云变幻、沧海桑田"作为次要信息,且语意重复,译文将其缩减为"relentless change"置于介词 of 之后来修饰"a century",符合英语叙述习惯。第三部分的主语为"追求",第四部分的主语为"初心",但二者皆是对中国青年的描述,并且该文的主体为中国青年,故译文将"中国青年"设定为主语,"始终未改"及"始终未变"作为谓语,因为两个谓语语义相同,故合并翻译为"have never wavered in… nor in",顾及英语的行文便利,增强了译文的可读性。

6. 首先,"新民主主义革命时期"在译文中增加了具体的时间信息"(1919—1949)",有利于读者更准确地理解源语概念,增强译文的可读性。其次,"中国青年"译为"they"而非"China's youth"有利于增强译文的衔接性,符合英语的行文习惯,增强了译文的可读性。再次,该句四字格居多,如"不怕牺牲、敢于斗争……民族独立、人民解放,冲锋陷阵、抛洒热血",除信息功能外,语言的表情功能较强,译文着重再现原文的信息功能,将"不怕牺牲、敢于斗争"译为"without fear of death","民族独立、人民解放"译为"national independence and the people's liberation","冲锋陷阵、抛洒热血"译为"fought bravely for",语义内容完整。最后,该句凸显汉语重意合的特点,在各个部分之间并无明显的逻辑衔接词,而译文用 and 将"rose to the occasion without fear of death"和" fought bravely for national independence and the people's liberation"进行衔接,凸显了英语重形合的特点。

7. 首先,"在社会主义革命和建设时期"在译文中添加了时间背景信息,有利于英语读者更好地理解原文信息。其次,因英语多使用代词指代进行衔接,故该句中"中国青年"的处理方式与上一句相同,将其翻译为"they"。再次,该句四字格使用较多,且在该语境下的语意近似,如"勇于拼搏""发奋图强""甘于奉献"及"忘我劳动",译文将其统一处理为"dedicated themselves to",有利于保障译文的流畅及简洁。

8. 首先,"中国青年"在本段中已是第四次出现,第一次出现时,将其翻译为"China's youth",第二次和第三次出现时,均翻译为"they",第四次出现将其翻译为"those",有助于增强译文衔接手法的多样性及译文的可读性。其次,"开拓创新、勇立潮头"在译文中处理为 who 引导的定语从句,将"锐意改革、拼搏奋进"翻译为主句的谓语动词,突出了中国青年的时代形象,逻辑清晰、主次分明,符合英语的行文习惯。

9. 首先,译文中添加了党的十八大召开的时间信息,有利于读者更好地理解原文,获得与源语读者相同的时间概念。其次,国际社会高度关注十八大的召开,认为十八大的召开是一个标志性的时刻,译文的谓语动词"mark"凸显了十八大的重要意义。

10. 首先,该句由五部分构成,叙述层次较为复杂。译文根据句间逻辑关系,将该句进行拆译。第一个小句和第五个小句分别翻译为两个独立的句子,有利于增强译文的流畅性及可读性。其次,"高度重视青年、热情关怀青年、充分信任青年"中重复出现"青年"一词,如果译文不做任何改变,将其译为 youth 或者 young people,译文会变得不够简洁,不符合英语的行文习惯,因此译文将第二个和第三个"青年"处理为代词"them",增强了译文的衔接性。再次,"鲜明提出""大力倡导""着力发挥"三组四字词均表明其后的内容是党中央的工作重点,语义功能相似,故将其译为"It is committed that …"。最后,汉语重意合,注重语意连贯而非结构完整,会出现承接前句主语的现象。根据语义逻辑判断,"推动青年发展事业实现全方位进步、取得历史性成就"的逻辑主语是"党中央",因此译文中添加代词"This"进行前指,符合英语重形合的语言特质,确保了译文的准确性。

11. 首先,该句中"展现"与"迸发"语义相近,译文将其合并为一个词进行翻译。其次,"亮丽的青春风采"与"豪迈的青春激情"是一对平行结构,译文中将其统一处理为形容词加名词的结构,有利于再现原文的行文特色。

12. 该句叙述层次十分复杂,语言信息相当丰富。首先,根据叙事逻辑,该句被拆分为三个独立的完整句:第一句描写中国青年的特质,在译文中独立成句;第二句说明中国青年与中国共产党的关系,在译文中同样独立成句;最后一句由几个分句构成,描写了中国青年的风貌,在译文中处理为一个长句。整体而言,译文语言信息完整、语言逻辑清晰,符合译入语的行文习惯。其次,原文中,"刚健自信、胸怀天下、担当有为"既传达了语言信息,又表现出语言美,译文表达为"confident, aspirant and responsible",着重再现其语言信息。再次,"衷心拥护党的领导"独立成句后,添加了逻辑主语"they"来指代中国青年,符合英语重形合的特点。然后,将第三个小句翻译为主句,并添加逻辑主语"they",确保了英语句式结构的完整性。同时,根据语言逻辑,译文将"展现出前所未有的昂扬风貌"处理为介词短语,作为状语对主语"they"进行修饰,根据叙述层次,将冒号后的内容处理为非谓语动词,对主语进行进一步解释说明,语言衔接流畅自然,逻辑层次清晰明了,符合英语的行文特点。另外,根据英语词汇搭配,"信仰"与"信念"在译文中合译为"belief","时刻彰显着鲜明的爱国主义精神气质"与"深植家国情怀,与国家同呼吸、与人民共命运"语义近似,因此译文中未出现该句的翻译。

13. 首先,该句由四个小句构成,前两个小句说明中国共产党对中国青年的重要意义,在译文中独立成句;后两个小句在结构上相近,在语义上递进,在译文中处理为另一个独立的句子。

14. 首先,原文中的"在庆祝中国共产党成立100周年大会上"作为状语位于主谓之间,符合汉语重意合的特点,但该语段内容较多,在英文中如果依然置于主谓之间则会影响译文行文的流畅性。因此,译文按照英语语言规范,将该部分作为状语前置于句首,有利于拉近主谓之间的结构距离。其次,源语小句间的逻辑关系呈现隐形,翻译时将"实现中华民族伟大复兴"及"增强做中国人的志气、骨气、底气"处理为非谓语动词,并添加衔接词 and 及 so that,符合英语重形合的要求。最后,"不负时代,不负韶华,不负党和人民的殷切期望!"是习近平总书记对中国青年提出的要求,其中,"不负时代"是社会层面的要求,"不负韶华"是个人层面的要求,"不负党和人民的殷切期望"是国家层面的要求。按照不同次序,译文将其进行适当调整,先翻译个人要求,其次是社会要求,最后是国家要求,符合英语叙述逻辑。

15. 首先,该句是全文的结束句,表示对中国青年不断奋斗充满信心,因此该译文以"will keep on striving"作为谓语动词。其次,"永不懈怠的精神状态、永不停滞的前进姿态",语言结构对称,有助于抒发情感,译文着重处理其语义概念,将对称的语言结构简化为"with boundless energy",符合英语信息型文本的语言特点。

参考译文:

Youth of China in the New Era

Youth is the most active and vital force in society. The hopes of a country and the future of a nation lie in the hands of its young generation. Young Chinese have always played a vanguard role in the quest for national rejuvenation.

After 1840, China was gradually reduced to a semi-colonial, semi-feudal society and suffered enormous hardships. The country endured intense humiliation, the people were subjected to great pain, and China's civilization was plunged into darkness. China's youth gradually came to recognize the mounting national crisis.

The enlightenment of its youth lit a beacon of hope for the rejuvenation of the Chinese nation. Around the May Fourth Movement in 1919, a large number of aspiring and progressive young intellectuals assumed the lead in accepting new ideas, new culture, and new knowledge. After careful consideration they chose to follow Marxism-Leninism, which led to a widespread awakening of the people and the nation for the first time since the Opium War. In July 1921, 13 delegates, of an average age of only 28, participated in the first National Congress of the Communist Party of China (CPC) and announced the founding of the Party, an epoch-making event that sounded the clarion call for the awakening and rise of the nation. This marked the beginning of a new era of national rejuvenation for China. Under the CPC's leadership, the Communist Youth League of China (CYLC) was established in 1922, opening a new chapter of the Chinese youth movement.

Looking back on a century of relentless change, China's youth have never wavered in their determination to love the Party, the country and the people, nor in their commitment to the original aspiration of following the instructions and guidance of the Party. During the New Democratic Revolution (1919-1949), they rose to the occasion without fear of death and fought bravely for national independence and the people's liberation. During the socialist revolution and reconstruction (1949-1978), they endured hardships and dedicated themselves to building the newly-founded country. In the new period of reform, opening up and socialist modernization, those with a talent for innovation who were open to challenges stood out and forged ahead, led reform, and ensured that China progressed with the times.

The 18th CPC National Congress held in 2012 marks the beginning of a new era in the development of socialism with Chinese characteristics. The CPC Central Committee with Comrade Xi Jinping at its core attaches great importance to young people, and cares deeply about them, and fully trusts them. It is committed to the principle that the Party exercises leadership over youth, gives top priority to youth development, and ensures the CYLC plays its role to the full as an aide to the Party and a reserve force. This will enable the younger generations to develop fully and achieve historic progress. In this great new era, China's youth have shown amazing vibrancy and great passion.

Young Chinese people in the new era are confident, aspirant and responsible. They wholeheartedly support the leadership of the Party. With a global vision, they stand at the forefront of the times bursting with commitment: pursuing lofty ideals with a firm belief in Marxism, communism and socialism with Chinese characteristics; full of patriotism, sharing weal and woe with the country and the people; displaying the sterling quality of living up to responsibilities; being the first in the country to worry about the affairs of the state and the last to enjoy themselves; striving to be pioneers in, pacesetters for and contributors to the country's development.

History shows clearly that without the CPC, the Chinese youth movement would have achieved little. For China's youth, commitment to the CPC is the most valuable experience, and the revolutionary traditions passed down are the most precious wealth accumulated over the past century.

In his speech addressing a ceremony celebrating the CPC centenary on July 1, 2021, Xi Jinping, general secretary of the CPC Central Committee, emphasized that "In the new era, our young people should make it their mission to contribute to national rejuvenation and aspire to become more proud, confident, and assured in their identity as Chinese people, so that they can live up to the promise of their youth and the expectations of our times, our Party and our people."

We have stood at a new historical starting point and embarked on a new journey in achieving the rejuvenation of the Chinese nation. Looking ahead to the new era, China's youth are embracing precious opportunities to realize their ambitions and display their talents, as they shoulder the important responsibility of building a great modern socialist country and realizing the Chinese Dream of national rejuvenation.

The Chinese Dream is a dream about history, the present and the future. It is cherished by all of the people, but even more so by the young. China's youth in the new era will keep on striving with boundless energy, to turn the Chinese Dream of national rejuvenation into reality. (China Daily online, 2022)

2. 中国的粮食安全

中国人口占世界的近1/5，粮食产量约占世界的1/4。①中国依靠自身力量端牢自己的饭碗，实现了由"吃不饱"到"吃得饱"，并且"吃得好"的历史性转变。②这既是中国人民自己发展取得的伟大成就，也是为世界粮食安全作出的重大贡献。③

当前，中国粮食连年丰收、库存充裕、供应充足、市场稳定，粮食安全形势持续向好。④展望未来，中国有条件、有能力、有信心依靠自身力量筑牢国家粮食安全防线。国家粮食安全保障政策体系基本成型，全面实施国家粮食安全战略，依靠自己保口粮，集中国内资源保重点，使粮食之基更牢靠、发展之基更深厚、社会之基更稳定。⑤农业供给侧结构性改革尚有很大空间，粮食科技进步、单产提高、减少损失浪费、利用非粮食食物等方面还有较大潜力可供挖掘。⑥充足的粮食储备可以保障粮食市场供应和市场基本稳定，现代化的粮食仓储物流体系可以防止出现区域性阶段性粮食供给紧张的问题，市场机制充分发挥作用能够解决品种结构矛盾。

从中长期看，中国的粮食产需仍将维持紧平衡态势，确保国家粮食安全这根弦一刻也不能放松。从需求形势看，随着经济社会发展，人均口粮消费将稳中略降，饲料和工业转化用粮消费继续增加，粮食消费总量刚性增长，粮食消费结构不断升级。⑦从生产形势看，农业生产成本仍在攀升，资源环境承载能力趋紧，农业基础设施相对薄弱，抗灾减灾能力有待提升，在确保绿色发展和资源永续利用的同时，稳定发展粮食生产压力较大。⑧从流通形势看，粮食生产将继续向核心产区集中，跨区域粮食流通量将进一步增加，粮食市场大幅波动的风险依然存在。⑨

展望世界粮食安全形势，国际粮农机构全球粮食安全治理效果逐步显现，各国促进国际粮食市场有序流通、维护世界粮食市场总体稳定的愿望增强，贫困缺粮国家粮食生产得到发展，能够减轻国际市场波动对国内市场带来的不利影响，为中国和世界粮食安全营造良好环境。⑩与此同时，当今世界粮食安全挑战依然严峻，仍有8亿多饥饿人口，国际粮食贸易面临着保护主义和单边主义的干扰，不稳定因素增加，实现相关可持续发展目标任重道远。⑪

立足国内，放眼全球，中国将继续坚定不移地走中国特色粮食安全之路，全面贯彻新发展理念，全面实施国家粮食安全战略和乡村振兴战略，全面落实"藏粮于地、藏粮于技"战略，推动从粮食生产大国向粮食产业强国迈进，把饭碗牢牢端在自己手上，在确保国家粮食安全的同时，与世界各国携手应对全球饥饿问

题,继续在南南合作框架下为其他发展中国家提供力所能及的帮助,共同推进全球粮食事业健康发展。⑫(中国日报网,2019)

词汇:

粮食安全 food security

世界人口 the world population

依靠自己保口粮 food self-sufficiency

供给侧结构性改革 supply-side structural reform

非粮食食物 non-grain foods

粮食仓储物流体系 grain storage and logistics system

区域性阶段性粮食供给紧张 regional or provisional food supply crises

市场机制 market mechanisms

工业转化用粮 grain used for industrial purposes

农业生产成本 agricultural costs

资源环境承载能力 resource and environmental carrying capacity (RECC)

农业基础设施 agricultural infrastructure

抗灾减灾能力 capacity for disaster prevention and relief

绿色发展 green development

资源永续利用 sustainable resource use

核心产区 core production areas

跨区域粮食流通量 transregional grain flows

国际粮农机构 international institutions for food and agriculture

全球粮食安全治理 global food security governance

保护主义 protectionism

单边主义 unilateralism

国家粮食安全战略 national strategies for food security

乡村振兴战略 national strategies for rural vitalization

南南合作框架 the framework of South-South cooperation

翻译解析:

1. 源语中的各小句之间没有使用任何衔接词汇,句子结构松散,字里行间的逻辑关系较为隐匿。根据标题判断,第一个小句为铺垫信息,译为介词短语作状语,第二个小句为主要信息,译为主句,译文主次信息明确,既符合源语语言逻辑又符合译入语行文习惯。

2."吃不饱""吃得饱""吃得好"为对仗结构，而且押韵，译文在处理时，放弃了结构及音韵特征，主要将"中国人民不仅仅有足够的食物，而且选择较多"这一概念表达出来，以突出信息型文本的特征。

3.根据叙述层次，"发展"作为方式状语译为"through hard work and development"。该句在译文中进行了分译，以突出中国粮食产量历史性转变的伟大成就及为世界粮食安全作出的贡献。

4.该句在译文中进行了拆译，将"当前，中国粮食连年丰收"翻译为独立的句子。对"库存充裕、供应充足、市场稳定"采用 there be 句型进行翻译，符合源语的语义需求，"粮食安全形势持续向好"是根据库存、供应及市场情况进行的总结，译为"increasing food security"，在定语从句中作介宾结构。

5.首先，该句由五个小句构成，根据叙述层次，可译为两个独立句，原文中的第一个小句说明国家粮食安全保障政策体系已基本建立，在译文中独立成句；原文中的剩余小句说明全国的粮食安全战略是什么，根据逻辑关系译作另一个独立句。其次，"依靠自己保口粮，集中国内资源保重点，使粮食之基更牢靠、发展之基更深厚、社会之基更稳定"是对"全面实施国家粮食安全战略"内容的解释，根据该语义逻辑，译文选择"consist of"作为谓语动词。最后，"使粮食之基更牢靠、发展之基更深厚、社会之基更稳定"的语言结构对称，在传递信息的同时达到了修辞的目的。就语义逻辑而言，"粮食之基""发展之基"与"社会之基"属递进关系，其中"粮食之基"是基础，因此，根据该语义逻辑，译文处理为"securing food supply as a foundation for national development and social stability"。

6.首先，该句的主要信息为"有很大空间"及"有较大潜力"，译文采用两个"there be"句型进行翻译，准确再现源语信息重点。其次，就逻辑关系而言，"单产提高、减少损失浪费、利用非粮食食物等方面"是对"粮食科技进步"涉及领域的具体说明。英文讲求逻辑关系的严密性，因此"单产提高、减少损失浪费、利用非粮食食物等方面"译为"in terms of increasing per unit area yield, reducing food waste, and developing non-grain foods"，准确再现这一逻辑关系。

7.首先，根据叙述层次，该句可分为三个部分。第一部分主要说明人均口粮消费情况，第二部分说明饲料及工业用粮情况，第三部分说明粮食消费总量及结构情况。据此，译文将该句翻译为三个小句并用分号进行衔接。其次，原文最后两个小句介绍粮食消费的总体情况，译文将其主语统一设定为"total grain consumption",语言结构清晰,行文流畅简洁。

8. 该句从"农业生产成本""资源环境承载能力""农业基础设施""抗灾减灾能力""粮食生产压力"五方面介绍粮食生产形势。译文中,"农业生产成本仍在攀升"与"资源环境承载能力趋紧"用 and 进行并列,并独立成句。"农业基础设施相对薄弱"与"抗灾减灾能力有待提升"同样使用 and 进行并列,并独立成句。根据逻辑关系,"在确保绿色发展和资源永续利用的同时"被译作由 while 引导的状语从句,主句为"稳定发展粮食生产压力较大",该小句为主题显著句型,主题为"稳定发展粮食生产压力",述题为"较大",但英语属于主语显著语言,承受压力的主体是中国,因此译文将主语译为"China",符合英语行文习惯。

9. 根据叙述层次,该句拆分为两个独立的句子。译文中,后两个小句用并列连词 and 衔接,符合英语的行习惯。

10. 首先,该句主要介绍国际粮农机构取得的成绩、各国的意愿,以及贫困缺粮国家的粮食生产情况与作用。据此,该句在译文中被拆分为三个独立句,语言明确、逻辑清晰。其次,"促进国际粮食市场有序流通、维护世界粮食市场总体稳定"作为前置定语修饰限定"愿望",在译文中处理为 to do 不定式作"will"的后置定语,符合英语的语法规范。再次,"能够减轻国际市场波动对国内市场带来的不利影响,为中国和世界粮食安全营造良好环境"作为"贫困缺粮国家粮食生产得到发展"的结果状语,译文将其处理为 which 引导的非限定性定语从句,语言结构合理,语义完整。

11. 首先,该句没有使用明显的衔接词,主要靠语义进行衔接。译文添加了不同的衔接方式,如衔接词 while、and,非谓语动词 suffering、showing、to go、reaching 等,以更好地将重意合的汉语转化为重形合的英语。其次,该句内涵三层信息:第一,总说当今世界粮食安全面临严峻的挑战;第二,具体介绍忍饥挨饿的人数、保护主义和单边主义的干扰,以及存在的不稳定因素;第三,相关目标受到影响。据此,该句在译文中拆分为三个独立句,语言结构清晰,语义重点明确。

12. 整个段落由一个长句构成,主语"中国"只出现一次,且小句之间鲜有衔接词,凸显汉语重意合的特点。首先,"立足国内,放眼全球,中国将继续坚定不移地走中国特色粮食安全之路"说明中国走粮食安全之路的决心,在译文中独立成句;"全面实施国家粮食安全战略和乡村振兴战略"在译文中独立成句,"全面贯彻新发展理念"及"全面落实'藏粮于地、藏粮于技'战略"分别译作非谓语动词及介词短语作状语,符合英语重形合的特点。其次,"推动从粮食生产大国向粮食产业强国迈进,把饭碗牢牢端在自己手上"介绍了中国在粮食生产方面取得的成绩,在译文中独立成句。再次,"在确保国家粮食安全的同时,与世界各国携手应对全球饥饿问题"说明中国与世界各国合作解决饥饿问题,在译文中独立成句。最后,"继续在南南合作框架下为其他发展中国家提供力所能及的帮助,共同推进全球粮食事业健康发展"在译文中独立成句;根据英语行文习惯,"在南南合作框架下"调整至该小句的末尾;小句之间添加并列连词 and 进行衔接,符合英语重形合的语言特点。

参考译文:

Food Security in China

With one fifth of the world population, China accounts for a quarter of total global food production. China is self-reliant in securing its own food supply; its people now have not only enough to eat, but also a greater range of choices. Compared to past times when they were underfed, this historical change has been made possible by the Chinese themselves through hard work and development. It is also a key contribution to world food security.

China has recently enjoyed a run of good harvests. There are adequate grain supplies and reserves, and a stable grain market, which are indicators of increasing food security. Looking to the future, China has the conditions, capabilities and confidence to enhance food security relying on its own efforts. A national system of food security guarantee policies is in place. China's food strategy in the new era consists of ensuring security of food through food self-sufficiency, pooling domestic resources to ensure key links in food security, and securing food supply as a foundation for national development and social stability. There is plenty of space for supply-side structural reform in China's agriculture industry; there is plenty of room for progress in China's agro-technology, in terms of increasing per unit area yield, reducing food waste, and developing non-grain foods. Adequate grain reserves help ensure market supply and a basically stable market; a modernized grain storage and logistics system helps prevent regional or provisional food supply crises; market mechanisms in full play help improve the structure of grain varieties.

In the medium to long term, China's grain production and demand will remain closely aligned, which means China must not slacken its efforts to ensure food security.

Per capita grain consumption and demand will drop slightly with social and economic development; the consumption of grain as feed for livestock and grain used for industrial purposes will continue to rise; total grain consumption will increase and pursue higher quality. In terms of grain production, agricultural costs are still rising, and resource and environmental carrying capacity (RECC) is broaching its limit. Agricultural infrastructure is comparatively weak, and capacity for disaster prevention and relief must be improved. China will find itself under considerable pressure to maintain steady grain production while ensuring green development and sustainable resource use. In terms of grain circulation, grain production will continue to be concentrated in core production areas. Transregional grain flows will increase, and there is still the risk of dramatic fluctuations in the grain market.

In global terms, international institutions for food and agriculture have achieved outcomes in improving global food security governance. All countries have an increasing will to facilitate orderly circulation in the international food market and overall stability. Progress has been made in grain production in low-income food-deficit countries, which will mitigate the negative impact of international market fluctuations upon domestic markets, and create a sound environment for China's and for global food security. At the same time, today's world is still facing severe food security challenges. There are still over 800 million people suffering from hunger, while international food trade is being disrupted by protectionism and unilateralism, and showing increasing instability. These challenges mean that the world has a long way to go in reaching its sustainable development goals.

In view of domestic and global food security, China will forge ahead along its own path. Pursuing a new development philosophy, China will implement its national strategies for food security and rural vitalization through sustainable farmland use and agricultural technology innovation to increase farmland productivity. China will advance from a large grain producer to a food industry power, holding firm its "rice bowl". While ensuring domestic food security, China will join the global fight against hunger. China will continue to provide assistance to the best of its ability to other developing countries within the framework of South-South cooperation, and promote the sound development of the global food industry. (China Daily online, 2019)

3. 元宵节的起源

农历正月十五日是元宵节,紧随春节之后。古时候,人们提前二十天为"春节"做准备,然而,元宵节为春节画上了句号,元宵之后,一切归于平常。

"元"是第一的意思,"宵"指夜晚。元宵就是新年首个夜晚,元宵节是家庭团聚的传统佳节,最隆重的活动就是展挂各种各样美丽的灯笼,故此,元宵节又叫"灯节"。①

关于元宵节的起源之说多种多样,但是最确切的一种说它跟宗教信仰有关。

有这样一个传说,元宵节是拜"太乙"神的日了,太乙是古代的天神。古人认为天神掌管着人类世界的命运,太乙手下有九条龙听他使唤,他决定人间什么时候遭遇饥荒瘟疫之祸,什么时候受旱灾水涝之苦。②从统一中国的第一个皇帝秦始皇开始,每年都举行盛大的仪式,皇帝祈求"太乙"神赐予他和臣民们风调雨顺、健康长寿。③汉武帝对元宵灯会特别重视,元封七年(公元前104年),他把元宵钦定为最重要的佳庆之一,庆祝仪式通宵进行。④

另一个传说认为"灯节"与道教有关。"天官"是道教的神,专管人间祥运,他出生于农历正月十五。相传"天官"喜乐,所以他的信徒们就准备各种各样的活动,祈求好运。

还有一种传说认为元宵节与佛教有关。⑤东汉明帝时期,佛教进入中国,这也是佛教首次传入中国,然而,佛教并没有对中国人产生多大影响。⑥一日,明帝做了个梦,梦见皇宫里有个金人,正当他准备问清这个神秘人物的身世时,金人突然升入天空,消失在西面。⑦次日,明帝委派一位学士去印度开始了他的取经之旅,经过几千里的长途跋涉,学士终于带回了经卷。汉明帝下令建造一所寺庙供佛雕安身、收藏经书。佛徒们相信佛能驱走黑暗,所以汉明帝宣昭他的臣民们张灯结彩,这样就形成了"灯节"。

张灯的习俗得以延续传承,然而,灯盏由简朴到华贵,样式繁多,庆贺的规模也愈来愈大。(中国日报网,2014)

词汇:

元宵节 the Yuanxiao Festival

农历 Chinese lunar month

春节 the Spring Festival

家庭团聚 family reunion

灯节 the Lantern Festival
宗教信仰 religious worship
风调雨顺 favorable weather
健康长寿 good health
汉武帝 Emperor Wudi of the Han Dynasty
道教 Taoism
佛教 Buddhism
明帝 Emperor Mingdi

翻译解析：

1. 首先，该句根据叙述层次在译文中被拆分为四个独立的句子。其次，"元宵就是新年首个夜晚"是指元宵节是新年过后的第一个月圆之夜，据此，该句译为"Yuanxiao is the first time when we see the full moon in the New year"。最后，"元宵节"在该句中重复两次出现，在译文中分别译作"It"和"the occasion"，通过代词及定冠词加名词进行指代，符合英语的行文习惯。

2. 根据叙述层次，该句在译文中被拆分为三个独立的句子。"他决定人间什么时候遭遇饥荒瘟疫之祸，什么时候受旱灾水涝之苦"在译文中采用强调句以突出"太乙"天神。原句中两次出现"什么时候"，译文只翻译了一次，确保行文的简洁。

3. 首先，该句在译文中被拆分为两个独立的句子，以确保逻辑结构明晰、语言信息完整。其次，"统一中国的第一个皇帝"是对"秦始皇"的解释说明，译文将其后置于"Qinshihuang"之后作同位语，符合英语的语言习惯。再次，"每年都举行盛大的仪式"属于典型的意合句式，缺省主语。译文根据语义逻辑添加主语"all subsequent emperors"，确保译文语言结构的完整性。

4. 首先，根据叙述层次，该句在译文中被拆分为两个独立的句子。其次，前文已将"元宵节"译作"the Lantern Festival"，因此，"元宵灯会"译作"this event"进行指代，符合英语的衔接习惯。最后，"元封七年"作为时间状语并未出现在译文中，取而代之的是其后的补充信息，此处有助于英语读者快速定位时间，以免带来不必要的阅读压力，妨碍译文的流畅度及可读性。

5. "还有一种传说"并未机械地译作"still another legend"，而是处理为"The third story"，有利于更好地实现篇章衔接，使逻辑关系更加明晰，增强了译文的可读性。该句中的"佛教"一词并未出现在译文中，有利于避免 Buddhism 在本段频繁出现,影响译文的可读性。

6.首先,根据叙述层次,该句在译文中被拆分为三个独立的句子。其次,"这也是佛教首次传入中国"旨在说明佛教在汉明帝时期首次传入中国。英语读者可能对汉明帝的相关信息较少了解,不了解具体时间,阅读时难以捕捉联想意义,因此译文增添时间信息"That was in the first century",补充了读者缺失的背景信息,有利于加强译文的可读性。

7.首先,根据叙述层次,该句在译文中被拆分为两个独立的句子,分别介绍汉明帝和金人。其次,译文中适当运用了形合手法,如"his""and",符合英语的行文规范。

参考译文:

Yuanxiao Festival

The Yuanxiao Festival is on the 15th day of the first Chinese lunar month. It is closely related to the Spring Festival. In the old days, people began preparing for the Spring Festival about 20 days before. However, the Yuanxiao Festival marks the end of the New Year celebrations. And after the Yuanxiao Festival, everything returns to normal.

Yuan literally means first, while *Xiao* refers to night. Yuanxiao is the first time when we see the full moon in the New year. It is traditionally a time for family reunion. The most prominent activity of the Yuanxiao Festival is the display of all types of beautiful lanterns. So the occasion is also called the Lantern Festival.

There are many beliefs about the origin of the Lantern Festival. But one thing for sure is that it had something to do with religious worship.

One legend tells that it was a time to worship Taiyi, the God of Heaven in ancient times. The belief was that the God of Heaven controlled the destiny of the human world. He had nine dragons at his back and call. It was him who decided when to inflict drought, storms, famine or pestilence upon human beings. Beginning with Qinshihuang, the first emperor uniting the country, all subsequent emperors ordered splendid ceremonies each year. The emperor would ask Taiyi to bring favorable weather and good health to him and to his people. Emperor Wudi of the Han Dynasty directed special attention to this event. In 104 BC, he proclaimed it one of the most important celebrations and the ceremony would last throughout the night.

Another legend associated with the Lantern Festival is Taoism. Tianguan is the Taoist god responsible for good fortune. His birthday falls on the 15th day of the first lunar month. It is said that Tianguan likes all types of entertainment. So his followers prepare various kinds of activities during which they pray for good fortune.

The third story about the origin of the festival goes like this. Buddhism first entered China during the reign of Emperor Mingdi of the Eastern Han Dynasty. That was in the first century. However, it did not exert any great influence among the Chinese people. One day, Emperor Mingdi had a dream about a gold man in his palace. At the very moment when he was about to ask the mysterious figure who he was, the gold man suddenly rose to the sky and disappeared in the west. The next day, Emperor Mingdi sent a scholar to India on a pilgrimage to locate Buddhist scriptures. After journeying thousands of miles, the scholar finally returned with the scriptures. Emperor Mingdi ordered that a temple be built to house a statue of Buddha and serve as a repository for the scriptures. Followers believe that the power of Buddha can dispel darkness, so Emperor Mingdi ordered his subjects to display lighted lanterns during what was to become the Lantern Festival.

The custom of lighting lanterns continued. However, the lanterns would develop from simple ones to those of various color and shape. The scale of the celebration also increased greatly. (China Daily online, 2014)

4. 作为中国文化"名片"的瓷器

在英文中,"中国"与"瓷器"是一个词,这说明,很早时欧洲人认识中国是和瓷器联系在一起的。①瓷器在 15 世纪时就传入欧洲,在中外交流中占有重要位置。德国卡赛尔郎德博物馆至今还藏有一件中国明代青瓷碗。②历史上,中国和亚、欧等地瓷器交易极为频繁,而且数量巨大。据今人研究,在 1602 年至 1682 年间,仅荷兰东印度公司贩运的中国瓷器就有一千六百多万件。瓷器以其优雅精致的品质,为中国赢得了好名声。在公元 17 至 18 世纪欧洲将中国理想化的思潮中,瓷器扮演着重要角色。③我们在当时风行欧洲的洛可可风格中,也多少可以看出以瓷器、园林为代表的"中国风"的影响。

瓷器是中国文明史上的重要物品。瓷器的前身是陶器,釉陶是瓷器产生的基础。④大约在公元 1 世纪时,中国就出现了瓷器。到了宋代(960—1279)瓷器进入了成熟期。⑤宋瓷代表中国瓷器的最高水平,当时有钧、定、官、哥、汝五大名窑,各窑的瓷器均具创造性,一直是后代模仿的对象。自元代开始,景德镇开始成为中国的瓷器中心。⑥

中国瓷器莹然可玩,沉静的色彩、透明的胎体、优雅的图案、精巧的形状,都是一代一代瓷器艺人追求的目标。⑦青铜器、陶器、瓷器都是中国人喜爱之物,但风格各有不同。瓷器虽没有陶器的古朴,却多了一些细腻;没有青铜器那样肃穆,却多了一种轻巧和优雅。⑧

瓷器可以说是中国文化的名片,这个名片凝聚着中国文化的信息,也体现了中国人的审美追求。⑨(叶朗、朱良志《中国文化读本》)

词汇:

瓷器 porcelain

卡赛尔郎德博物馆 the Keisel Randy Museum

青瓷碗 blue-and-white bowl

荷兰东印度公司 the Dutch East India Company

洛可可风格 the rococo style

陶器 pottery

釉陶 glazed pottery

青铜器 bronzeware

审美追求 aesthetic pursuit

翻译解析：

1. 首先，根据叙述层次，该句在译文中可拆分两个独立的句子。其次，根据语义概念，"中国"译作"the country"，避免 China 一词在译文中重复出现，有利于增强译文的可读性。

2. "至今"作为时间概念译作一般现在时，而非具体的单词，翻译方法灵活，符合译文语言规范。"中国明代青瓷碗"在译文中省略了"中国"一词，并且添加了"dating back to"介词短语以明示"明代"与"青瓷碗"的修辞逻辑关系。

3. 根据叙述逻辑，该句旨在解释瓷器"为中国赢得了好名声"，在译文中用 and 将其与上一句进行并列，逻辑关系显化，符合英语重形合的语言特征。

4. 该句逻辑关系松散，译文添加关系副词 while 对句间关系进行显化处理，符合英语的行文规范。

5. 根据叙述层次，该句与前一句介绍瓷器的发展，译文采用衔接词 and 将两个句子合并为一个独立的句子，并将"宋代(960—1279)瓷器进入了成熟期"中的"瓷器"一词译作代词"it"加强句内逻辑衔接。

6. "元代"在译文中处理为"the Yuan Dynasty（1206—1368）"，添加了时间背景信息，有利于英语读者准确定位时间概念。

7. 首先，该句结构松散，隐形的逻辑关系需要通过文本分析，挖掘字里行间的隐性逻辑关系并将其显性化处理，才可输出形式衔接明显且逻辑关系严密的英文文本。其次，"沉静的色彩、透明的胎体、优雅的图案、精巧的形状"，就语言结构而言，语言表达对称，译文中将其统一处理为形容词加名词的结构，力求再现原文的语言结构；就语义而言，均为中国瓷器吸引人的原因，译文添加介词"for"以明示该逻辑关系。最后，"一代一代瓷器艺人追求的目标"是对主语"中国瓷器"的补充说明，译文将其处理为同位语，并调整"一代一代瓷器艺人追求的"与"目标"的先后顺序，符合英语行文规范。

8. 该句通过对比瓷器与陶器、瓷器与青铜器，说明陶器和青铜器的特点及瓷器的优点。据此，译文通过 while 衔接陶器和青铜器的特点，并用转折连词 but 强调瓷器的优点，语言完整，结构显化，符合英语的行文习惯。

9. "瓷器可以说是中国文化的名片"与标题呼应，译文将其从原句中拆分出来，译作一个独立的句子。

参考译文：

Porcelain—Calling Card of Chinese Culture

In English, the country and "porcelain" share the same name—"China". This proves that Europeans have long known of China's relationship to porcelain. Porcelain found its way to Europe in the 15th century, occupying an important position in the exchanges between China and other countries. The Keisel Randy Museum in Germany houses a blue-and-white bowl dating back to the Ming Dynasty (1368–1644). Throughout history, China, along with other Asian countries, and Europe maintained a busy and vast trade in porcelain. From 1602 to 1682, the Dutch East India Company transported more than 16 million articles of porcelain to Europe. Porcelain garnered a good reputation for China for its sophistication and elegance, and played an important role in the wave of the European idealization of China during the 17th and 18th centuries. In the rococo style popular in Europe of that time, one could sense, from time to time, the influence of "Chinese vogue" represented by China's styles of porcelain and gardens.

Porcelain is of great significance in the history of Chinese civilization. Pottery was the predecessor of porcelain, while glazed pottery was the basis for the emergence of porcelain. Around the first century, porcelain production first emerged in China, and by the Song Dynasty (960–1279) it had become mature. Song-dynasty porcelain represented the acme of Chinese porcelain technique. Five famous kilns, the Jun, Ding, Guan, Ge, and Ru, were all creative and original in their respective products, and their porcelain ware has been imitated by later generations throughout the ages. In the Yuan Dynasty (1206–1368), Jingdezhen became the center of the Chinese porcelain industry.

Chinese porcelain is cherished for its serene color, crystal paste, graceful designs, and ingenious forms—a quest of generations of craftspeople. Bronzeware, pottery and porcelain are all popular with the Chinese people, though their styles vary widely. Pottery is simple and unsophisticated, while bronzeware suggests solemnity, but porcelain is the most exquisite and elegant.

Porcelain can be regarded as the calling card of Chinese culture. This calling card represents the crystallization of Chinese culture and the embodiment of the aesthetic pursuits of the Chinese people. (章思英 译)

5. 京剧脸谱的绚烂之美

中国的京剧舞台,呈现的是浓厚的色彩美,是一种错彩镂金的绚烂之美。①制造这种艺术氛围的除了京剧舞台的服装之外,脸谱起了很大的作用。②京剧脸谱不同于面具。面具是罩在人脸上的,可以摘下来,而脸谱是化妆时画在演员的脸上的。③

京剧的脸谱是五彩缤纷的图案,有红、紫、白、黄、黑、蓝、绿、粉红、灰、褐金、银等各种色彩,极其夸张而又极其艳丽。

脸谱主要是用在"净""丑"这两种角色的脸上。④"净"又称"花脸","丑"就是"丑角"。⑤

脸谱有两种用意。一种是表明剧中人的身份和性格。如"红脸"表示这个人忠勇,"黑脸"表示这个人粗豪,"白脸"表示这个人奸恶,脸上画"豆腐块"表示这个人是小人物,等等。⑥再一种用意是体现人们对这个角色的道德评价和审美评价,如可敬的、可恨的、崇高的、可笑的,等等。

脸谱除了这种含意外,它本身又具有一种色彩美、图案美。⑦这种色彩美、图案美作为形式美,相对独立出来也值得欣赏。⑧如张飞的"蝴蝶脸谱"就是显示性格和图案美高度统一的精品。⑨今天,很多民间工艺品(如风筝、面人、泥人、地毯、挂毯等)、招贴画、广告画、模特服装的设计采取京剧脸谱作为设计的元素,就是着眼于这种形式美。同时,京剧脸谱这种色彩美、图案美,又渲染了整个京剧舞台的五彩缤纷的绚烂之美。⑩(叶朗、朱良志《中国文化读本》)

词汇:

京剧 Peking Opera

脸谱 masks

净 jing

丑 chou or clown

花脸 male character

丑角 clown

红脸 red face

黑脸 black face

白脸 white face

民间工艺品 folk handicrafts

面人 dough figurine

泥人 clay figurine

翻译解析：

1. "错彩镂金"原指诗文的辞藻华丽，此处指色彩丰富艳丽，据此译文将其处理为"vivid, intense and glamorous"来修饰"resplendent color"。

2. 该句说明中国京剧错彩镂金的艺术氛围一部分来源于脸谱，译文将"脸谱"一词与下一段描写京剧脸谱的内容进行合并，译作"masks of exaggerated, dazzling designs, gleaming with reds, purples, whites, yellows, blacks, blues, greens, every diverse color imaginable"，语义完整、结构合理，更好地诠释了京剧脸谱的绚丽之美。

3. 该句介绍京剧脸谱与面具的差异，与篇章主题的关系较为松散，译文对其进行省略，以突出前一句的内容。

4. 该句介绍脸谱主要用于哪种角色，与下一段第一个句子的主语一致。译文将其译为过去分词，作为插入语来修饰限定下一段第一个句子的主语。

5. 该句是对"净"和"丑"的解释说明，译文将其语义进行重新分配，分别译作"male character"及"clown"，用并列连词or与"净""丑"进行衔接。

6. 该句是对京剧脸谱第一种用意的举例。其中，"脸上画'豆腐块'表示这个人是小人物"在译文中进行了省略。

7. 根据叙述层次，"它本身又具有一种色彩美、图案美"在译文中处理为主句。其中，"色彩美、图案美"结构对称，除具有传递信息的功能外，还加强了原文的可读性。这一组对称结构译为"art of beautiful colors and designs for aesthetic appreciation"，译文保留了源语的对称结构，在传达源语语义之外，努力实现形式对等。

8. 根据叙述层次，译文对该句进行了省略。

9. 首先，英语读者对"张飞"这一历史人物可能不了解或了解不多，译文添加了同位语对这位历史人物进行解释说明，以降低文化背景不足对译文理解产生的影响，增强了文化传播效果。

10. 根据叙述层次，译文调整了该句在段落中的顺序，使段落语言逻辑更加顺畅。

参考译文：

The Delights of Peking Opera Masks

China's Peking Opera radiates with the beauty of resplendent color—vivid, intense and glamorous. This artistic beauty comes not only from the costumes but also from the masks of exaggerated, dazzling designs, gleaming with reds, purples, whites, yellows, blacks, blues, greens, every diverse color imaginable.

Masks, applied to the two roles of the "jing" or "male character", and the "chou" or "clown", serve two purposes. One is to indicate the identity and character of the role. For example, a "red face" means the person is loyal and brave; a "black face" signifies the person is straightforward; a "white face" identifies the person as crafty and evil. The other purpose is to express people's appraisal of the roles from a moral and aesthetic point of view, such as respectable, hateful, noble, or ridiculous, etc.

Besides being evocative, Peking Opera masks are in and of themselves an art of beautiful colors and designs for aesthetic appreciation. For example, Zhang Fei, a heroic character from the Three Kingdoms Period (220-280), has a facial design in Peking Opera in the shape of a butterfly—a masterpiece perfectly combining personality and artistic design. The intriguing beauty of the color and design of Peking Opera masks adds to the attractive spectacle onstage. Many Chinese folk handicrafts (e.g., kites, dough and clay figurines, carpets, tapestries), posters, advertisements, and fashions adopt Peking Opera masks as a source element in their designs. （章思英 译）

6.年画：渲染过年的热闹气氛

春节是中国最重要的传统节日，一到春节，无论城市农村，家家户户都要张灯结彩庆贺。①张贴年画，是春节的重要节目，②用年画将家里布置得热热闹闹，增加过年的气氛。③

年画在内容上多表现祝福、吉祥和喜庆之意。如一幅广为流传的年画《连年有余》，画一个胖娃娃，天真活泼，怀里抱着一条大鲤鱼，手里拿着一束莲花。④"鱼"和"余"在汉字中读音相同，通过谐音，以表示生活富足，年年有余。⑤

中国幅员辽阔，年画的风格上也有不同。北方的年画最著名的要数天津的杨柳青，南方年画最著名的要数苏州的桃花坞。⑥

杨柳青是天津西南郊的一个村镇，三百多年前，这里就以制作年画出名，曾有过"家家点染、户户丹青"的历史。⑦杨柳青年画采用的是木版套印和手工彩绘相结合的方法，人们称之为"半印半画"，这也是它的重要特色。⑧它的制作方法是：先刻出木刻图案版样，然后印出图画，再用手工将纸上的轮廓描绘涂彩，最后装裱成画。⑨每一幅画都是由画师手工制作的，而不是批量的印刷品。它将版画中的刀法版味和手画的笔触感觉融合在一起，有一种独特的风味。⑩人们喜欢杨柳青年画，在很大程度上是喜欢它是手工制作的。

年画的喜庆气氛，在杨柳青年画中体现得最为充分。这里出品的年画清新活泼，具有浓郁的生活情调。如一幅《母子图》，画湖边的庭院，院子里有湖石假山、花卉，妈妈站在窗前，拿着扇子，招呼着窗外嬉戏的儿子。⑪胖胖的小家伙穿着小肚兜，一只手拿着一个小木棍，木棍的顶端有一只小鸟。一片祥和温暖的气氛，是一幅温情的生活画面。⑫

苏州的桃花坞年画则体现出江南纤巧细柔的特点，它采用传统水印木刻的方法来印制。⑬在选材上，桃花坞年画除了吸收民间故事外，还大量采用文人绘画的内容，其画面多儒雅清淡，风格上不似杨柳青年画那样浓艳，更强调清雅流畅。⑭桃花坞年画曾传到日本，影响了日本浮世绘的绘画。在三百多年前，桃花坞就注意吸收西方铜版的雕刻风格，注意阴影的处理。桃花坞年画中的仕女图以其形象清新美貌而著称，受到人们的喜爱。⑮（叶朗、朱良志《中国文化读本》）

词汇：

年画 New Year Pictures

春节 Spring Festival（or Chinese New Year）

连年有余 Surplus in Successive Years

木版套印 xylograph overprinting

手工彩绘 hand-painted color

半印半画 half printing half painting

江南 areas south of the lower reaches of the Yangtze River

水印木刻 watercolor block printing

儒雅清淡 scholarly and refined

翻译解析：

1. 根据叙述层次，该句在译文中进行了拆分。译文对"一到春节"这一已知信息进行了省略。

2. "春节"在本段中已是第三次出现，为了避免在译文中重复出现同义词组，已将其处理为"this celebration"，既避免了原词重复给译文带来的尴尬，又与前文实现了照应。

3. 该句缺省主语，译文根据叙述逻辑添加"people"作主语，"增加过年的气氛"译作 to do 不定式作目的状语。

4 根据叙述层次，译文将"胖"及"天真活泼"处理为形容词作定语修饰限定"娃娃"，"怀里抱着一条大鲤鱼，手里拿着一束莲花"处理为现在分词词组作定语。语言链接形式显化，结构合理，语义完整。

5. 首先，根据叙述层次，该句在译文中被拆译为两个独立的句子。其次，译文中增补了"在汉字中读音相同"的具体读音"yu"，有利于英语读者理解这里的谐音。再次，译文中增补了"以表示生活富足，年年有余"的逻辑主语 people，符合英语语法要求。最后，"生活富足，年年有余"四字格连用，语义相近，因此译文将其合译为"affluent lives"。

6. 根据语言逻辑，"杨柳青"及"桃花坞"是指杨柳青产和桃花坞产的年画，而非地点。据此，译文增译了"those produced in"及"those from"来指代年画，增强了译文的准确性。

7. 首先，根据叙述层次，"杨柳青是天津西南郊的一个村镇"在译文中独立成句。其次，最后一个小句在译文中处理为独立主格结构，叙述逻辑层次分明，结构合理，语义完整。

8. 首先，"这也是它的重要特色"在译文中转译为名词词组"distinctive feature"。其次，译文中增译了"establishing"一词，将原句逻辑层次显化处理，符合英语重形合的特点。

9. 译文将"先""然后""再""最后"处理为阿拉伯数字,符合英语的行文习惯。

10. 译文将该句进行拆分,将第一个小句处理为一个句子,用并列连词 and 与上一句进行合并,第二个小句被处理为介词短语,内嵌于下一个句子作原因状语。

11. 首先,根据叙述层次,该句在译文中被拆分为两个独立的句子。其次,根据逻辑关系,"院子里有湖石假山、花卉"在译文中作为定语从句修饰限定"庭院",引导词 inside which 显示主从句逻辑关系。最后,"站在窗前,拿着扇子,招呼着窗外嬉戏的儿子"是汉语中的连动句,译文将"站"作主句谓语动词,"拿"译作独立组主格,"招呼"译作现在分词词组,二者作为伴随状语,合理分解了汉语的连动句式。

12. 首先,该句缺省主语,译文根据逻辑关系添加"the whole picture"作主语。其次,"一片祥和温暖的气氛"及"温情的生活画面"合译为"an affectionate, loving atmosphere of family life",语义完整,结构合理,符合英语行文习惯。

13. "它采用传统水印木刻的方法来印制"在译文中处理为插入语,对主句进行解释说明。

14. 首先,译文根据叙述层次,将原句语义分为两个层次,即年画的主题与画面的艺术性,两个层次通过分号进行衔接。其次,"风格上不似杨柳青年画那样浓艳"译作介词短语"unlike the heavy and resplendent style of the Yangliuqing pictures",对主句进行解释说明,语言结构合理,层次分明,符合英语行文习惯。最后,"更强调清雅流畅"与"画面多儒雅清淡,风格上不似杨柳青年画那样浓艳"语义重复,因此在译文中进行了省略。

15. 根据叙述逻辑,"仕女图以其形象清新美貌而著称"是桃花坞年画"受到人们的喜爱"的原因状语,译文将其处理为过去分词作原因状语,语言层次分明,结构合理,符合英语的行文习惯。

参考译文:

New Year Pictures: Enhancing the Festive Atmosphere

Spring Festival (or Chinese New Year) is the most important traditional festival in China. People celebrate it with lanterns and streamers, no matter where they live, in the countryside or in the city. New Year pictures are an indispensable part of this celebration for each and every household. People put up New Year pictures in their homes to enhance the lively festive atmosphere.

New Year pictures symbolize good fortune, auspiciousness and festivity. A popular New Year picture entitled *Surplus in Successive Years* depicts: a cute plump baby holding a big carp in his arms and a bouquet of lotus flowers in his hand. Fish and "surplus" in Chinese have the same pronunciation (*yu*). Through the homophony of the two words, people express their wishes for affluent lives.

China is a country of vast territory, so the styles of New Year pictures vary from north to south. The northern New Year pictures are best represented by those produced in Yangliuqing in Tianjin Municipality, while in the south there are those from Taohuawu in Suzhou City, Jiangsu Province.

Yangliuqing is a small town located in the southwestern outskirts of Tianjin. About 300 years ago, its New Year pictures began to enjoy great fame, with every family adept at creating this particular genre of painting. Yangliuqing New Year pictures adopt the method of xylograph overprinting combined with hand-painted color, hence establishing its distinctive feature of "half printing, half painting." The process goes like this: carve designs out of wood; print the pictures; color the pictures; and mount the pictures. All pictures are handmade paintings rather than mass-produced products, and all evoke traces of the woodcut and the feel of brushwork. With exquisite craftsmanship, Yangliuqing New Year pictures are very popular with Chinese people.

The lively festive atmosphere is best reflected in the Yangliuqing New Year pictures. Fresh and effervescent, each picture reproduces an interesting scene from everyday life. For example, *Mother and Son* depicts a lakeside courtyard, inside which are rock formations and flowers. The mother stands at a window, fan in hand, calling out to her son frolicking outside. The plump son in a bellyband holds a wooden stick with a bird perching on it. The whole picture brims with an affectionate, loving atmosphere of family life.

Taohuawu New Year pictures, produced using traditional techniques of watercolor block printing, are characteristic of the delicate and gentle style in areas south of the lower reaches of the Yangtze River. Thematically, the pictures draw much from the paintings of literati as well as folk stories; while artistically, most are scholarly and refined, unlike the heavy and resplendent style of the Yangliuqing pictures. Taohuawu New Year pictures once spread to Japan and exerted a certain influence on Japanese ukiyoe paintings, or paintings from the "floating world." About 300 years ago, Taohuawu New Year pictures began learning from the style of Western bronze carvings, as well as the use of shadow. Celebrated for its pure and attractive images of women, Taohuawu New Year pictures enjoy great popularity among the Chinese people. (章思英 译)

7. 刺绣：十指下的春风

中国是丝绸的故乡，有很多与丝绸相关的艺术，刺绣就是其中的一种。①从事刺绣的多为女子，所以刺绣又被称为"女红"。刺绣在中国有数千年的历史，受到人们广泛的喜爱。刺绣可用来装饰衣物，如在衣服、被子、枕头等物品上绣上美丽的图案，也可制作成特别的饰品。②

中国宋代就有锦院和绣院，集中了大量的编织和刺绣的专业人才，推进了丝织和刺绣的水平。③明代大画家董其昌说：宋人之绣，针线细密，用绒只一二丝，用针如发细者为之，设色精妙，光彩射目。④刺绣上的山水、楼阁、人物、花鸟都极为生动。他赞叹说："十指春风，盖至此乎！"⑤董其昌说的"十指春风"这四个字，正是对我国刺绣艺术审美妙境的极好赞扬。⑥

中国有"四大名绣"，即苏州的苏绣、广东的粤绣、湖南的湘绣及四川的蜀绣，各种绣法不仅风格有差异，所选择的内容也有不同。⑦历史上有"苏绣猫，湘绣虎"的说法。粤绣擅长鸟类，以"百鸟朝凤"最有名，而蜀绣则擅长山水人物。⑧

在这其中，苏绣最负盛名。20世纪初，苏绣名手沈云芝的作品《意大利皇后爱丽娜像》，曾作为国家礼品赠送给意大利，受到了极高评价。⑨

苏绣主要产生于苏州一带，也包括扬州、无锡、常州等地的刺绣。苏州一带盛产丝绸，民风又以细腻著称，苏绣因而大盛，苏绣有以针作画、巧夺天工的美名。⑩近千年来，苏州一带从事刺绣的人很多，几乎女子长大了，个个都会刺绣，有"家家养蚕，户户刺绣"的说法。⑪据说苏州的高超艺人绣一双猫眼，要用二十多种颜色的丝线，千缠万绕，就是为了突出眼睛炯炯有神。（叶朗、朱良志《中国文化读本》）

词　汇：

刺绣 embroidery

女红 women's needlework

锦院 the Satin Academy

绣院 the Embroidery Academy

针线细密 fine close stitches

四大名绣 four most famous types of embroidery

百鸟朝凤 One Hundred Birds Worship the Phoenix

最负盛名 the greatest reputation

国家礼品 state gift
以针作画 using needles to draw pictures
巧夺天工 with superb craft surpassing nature
炯炯有神 brightness and vitality

翻译解析：

1. 根据叙述层次，译文将前两个小句用 and 进行并列，"刺绣就是其中的一种"译作非限定性定语从句，引导词为 one of which。译文语言结构合理，逻辑关系明晰，符合英语的行文习惯。

2. 首先，"刺绣"一词已在本段出现四次，根据英语的衔接习惯，可将其译为代词"it"与前文照应，加强译文的衔接性与可读性。其次，"绣上美丽的图案"即为"装饰"，因此译文省略该信息。

3. 根据叙述层次，译文将"中国宋代就有锦院和绣院"译作主句，"集中了大量的编织和刺绣的专业人才"译作 where 引导的定语从句来修饰限定"锦院和绣院"，"推进了丝织和刺绣的水平"译作 to do 不定式，作为从句中的结果状语，说明专业人才给丝织及刺绣发展带来的影响。译文语言逻辑明晰，叙述层次分明，语言结构合理，符合英语行文习惯。

4. 首先，"宋代大画家董其昌"增译为"Dong Qichang（1555—1636），a famous painter in Ming dynasty（1368—1644）"，增加了生平信息及朝代信息，有利于不了解中国文化的英语读者准确定位时间背景，有利于中国文化的有效传播。其次，原文中的间接引语在译文中转译为直接引语。再次，根据逻辑关系判断，"针线细密"是对"宋人之绣"的描述，译文添加动词 boast，将其处理为主谓宾句型，语义恰当、结构合理，既能凸显宋人之绣的优点，又符合英语行文习惯。然后，根据逻辑关系判断，"用绒只一二丝，用针如发细者为之"是对完成"宋人之绣"的具体描述，译文将其处理为过去分词做状语，语言层次明晰，结构合理。最后，"设色精妙，光彩射目"在译文中独立成句，其中"设色精妙"作为主句，"光彩射目"作为结果状语，句子衔接流畅自然，衔接方式明显，符合英语的行文习惯。

5. "十指春风"是指十根指头就像春天的风一样灵巧，该隐喻在译文中转化为明喻，译作"The ten fingers must be like the spring breeze"。

6. 根据叙述逻辑判断，该句主要说明"十指春风"是董其昌对我国刺绣的赞扬，该信息与前文内容多有重合，因此在译文中进行了省略。

7. 根据本句叙述层次，将"各种绣法不仅风格有差异，所选择的内容也有不同"在译文中处理为独立主格结构,作状语。

8. 根据逻辑关系,该句与前一句为并列关系,介绍苏绣、湘绣、粤绣、蜀绣最擅长的内容。据此,译文将其与前一句合译为一个句子,并省略谓语动词"擅长",以提升句子的衔接性和整体性。

9. 首先,"苏绣名手沈云芝"增译为"the celebrated Suzhou embroiderer Shen Yunzhi (birth and death dates unknown)",背景信息的增加既体现了译者的专业态度,又增加了译文的准确性。其次,根据语境信息,"受到了极高评价"在译文中进行了省略。

10. 首先,根据叙述层次,该句在译文中被拆译为两个独立的句子。其次,根据英语重形合的语言特征,翻译"苏州一带盛产丝绸,民风又以细腻著称"时,在译文中用并列连词 and 进行衔接。"细腻"是指"精益求精的工作态度",将其译为"their meticulous work style",这里的 their 有利于提升句子的衔接性。最后,根据叙述逻辑,将"苏绣有以针作画、巧夺天工的美名"译为独立主格结构作状语,以说明苏绣大盛的具体情况。

11. 根据逻辑关系,在译文中,将"苏州一带从事刺绣的人很多"与"几乎女子长大了,个个都会刺绣"用并列连词 and 进行衔接;"有'家家养蚕,户户刺绣'的说法"是前文内容的结果状语,译文添加关系副词 hence 以显化这一逻辑关系。衔接词的添加既符合源语逻辑关系,又符合英语重形合的特征。

参考译文:

Embroidery: Ten Fingers Like a Spring Breeze

China is home to silk and to a variety of arts related to silk, one of which is embroidery. Most embroiderers are women, hence the byname for embroidery is, "women's needlework." With a long history of several thousand years, embroidery has been a love of Chinese people. It is applied to adorn clothes, quilts and pillowcases, or a piece of embroidery work can be an ornament in itself.

As early as in the Song Dynasty (960–1279), China officially established the Satin Academy and the Embroidery Academy, where a great number of weaving and embroidery professionals gathered together to promote the standards of silk weaving and embroidery. Dong Qichang (1555–1636), a famous in painter Ming dynasty (1368–1644), commented, "Song-dynasty embroidery boasts fine close stitches, done with one or two types of silk thread and hair-thin needles. Colors are deftly and intriguingly applied, making the whole piece splendid to look at." The embroidered mountains, rivers, pagodas, figures, birds, and flowers are all vividly brought out. He was said to have sighed in admiration, "The ten fingers must be like the spring breeze, producing such vivid pictures!"

China has four most famous types of embroidery—respectively from Suzhou, Guangdong, Hunan, and Sichuan—each with its own style and different themes. Historically, Suzhou embroidery was famous for its cats, Hunan embroidery for its tigers, Guangdong embroidery for its birds (the most famous being *One Hundred Birds Worship the Phoenix*), and Sichuan embroidery for its landscapes and human figures.

Among the four styles, Suzhou embroidery has enjoyed the greatest reputation. In the early 20th century, *Portrait of an Italian Queen* by the celebrated Suzhou embroiderer Shen Yunzhi (birth and death dates unknown) was presented to Italy as a state gift.

Suzhou embroidery is produced mainly in the Suzhou area, in addition to Yangzhou, Wuxi and Changzhou. Suzhou is abundant in silk, and people here and in the surrounding areas are known for their meticulous work style. For these two reasons, embroidery has developed quickly, with Suzhou embroidery gaining the reputation of "using needles to draw pictures with superb craft surpassing nature." Over a period of nearly 1,000 years, a great number of Suzhou people have gone into embroidery and almost every girl grows up to be a capable embroiderer, hence the local saying "Every house raises silkworms, every home does embroidery." It is said that a skillful embroiderer uses silk thread of more than 20 colors for a cat's eyes, so as to achieve the effect of brightness and vitality. (章思英 译)

8. 皮影戏：灯和影的艺术

18世纪后半叶，法国曾经出现过一种叫作"法兰西灯影"的戏剧形式，在巴黎、马赛等地演出时引起轰动。①那是传教士将中国的皮影戏介绍到法国，法国的戏剧家在皮影戏的基础上创造出来的艺术形式。②有趣的是，在2004年的中法文化年期间，中国的艺术家又把一部新创作的皮影戏《影之舞》送到了法国。皮影戏记载着中外文化交流的历史。③

在世界历史上，要说中国文化对世界的影响，皮影戏是不可忽视的。④这种创自中国的戏剧形式，在13世纪就传到了中东，到了18世纪便有了世界性的影响。⑤皮影戏曾经受到歌德的赞扬，20世纪，卓别林的无声电影也受到了皮影戏的启发。⑥

皮影戏产生于两千多年前，到了宋代，皮影戏已十分发达，中国皮影戏的主要形式此时都具备了。⑦当时传统戏剧并没有成熟，但皮影戏已经相当成熟，利用皮影戏，可以演出完整的三国故事等。⑧当时很多城市都有皮影戏演出，节日的时候，皮影戏更成了重要的娱乐形式。明代仅北京一地，就有皮影戏戏班几十个。至今皮影戏仍然受到人们的喜爱。皮影戏是世界上最早由人配音的活动影画艺术，它的成功给现代电影以很大启发。⑨

皮影人物的制作非常考究。先将准备好的皮革，做成人的头、四肢、躯干等模样，再用绳索将其串起，用连杠连成一体，成为颜色鲜艳的人物形象。⑩在演出时，用灯光照射在皮革做成的人物上，形成活灵活现的剪影，通过他们的动作表演故事，若真若幻，赏心悦目。⑪

皮影戏的妙处不仅在于皮影的制作，更在于表演。表演时，几个表演者站在一块白布后面，操纵着各种形状的皮影人，同时演唱着故事，还配有打击乐器或弦乐。⑫陕西华县的皮影戏很有名，他们形象地称皮影戏为"五人忙"，五个人演了一台戏："前声"是负责唱的，一人要唱生旦净丑几个角色；"签手"负责操纵皮影进行表演；"坐槽"负责敲锣、打碗、打梆子等；"上档"负责拉二弦琴、吹唢呐；"下档"负责拉板胡、长号，并配合签手的工作。⑬五个人在台后忙翻了天，共同演出一出戏。

皮影戏表演水平的高低，取决于演员的唱功和"手功"。在幕后手提皮影可不是一件简单的事，往往一个皮影，要用五根竹棍操纵，要求演员手指灵活，好的演员常常能令观众眼花缭乱。⑭（叶朗、朱良志《中国文化读本》）

词汇：

皮影戏 Shadow Play

灯影 Light and Shadow

中法文化年 China-France Year of Culture

影之舞 The Dance of Shadows

无声电影 silent film

影戏戏班 shadow play troupe

影画艺术 movie art

皮影人物 shadow-play puppet

若真若幻 imagination mixed with reality

赏心悦目 delight both the eyes and hearts of the audience

打击乐器 percussions

弦乐 stringed musical instruments

五人忙 Five-person Event

锣 gongs

碗 bowls

梆子 percussions

二弦琴 the two-stringed fiddle

唢呐 trumpet

板胡 the banhu fiddle

长号 trombone

翻译解析：

1. 根据叙述层次，译文将"法国曾经出现过一种叫作'法兰西灯影'的戏剧形式"译作主句；"一时引起轰动"译作 which 引导的定语从句修饰限定"法兰西灯影"；"在巴黎、马赛等地演出时"译作 when 引导的时间状语从句，内嵌于定语从句，对其进行修饰。

2. 首先，根据逻辑关系判断，"传教士将中国的皮影戏介绍到法国，法国的戏剧家在皮影戏的基础上创造出来的"在原句中作为定语修饰限定"艺术形式"。根据英语行文习惯，将该定语置于中心词 an artistic form 之后进行翻译，避免了句子出现头重脚轻的情况。其次，这里的"皮影戏"特指由传教士介绍到法国的皮影戏。据此，译文调整了"传教士将中国的皮影戏介绍到法国"与"法国的戏剧家在皮影戏的基础上创造出来的"语言顺序,将"传教士将中国的皮影戏介绍到法国"译作过去分词作后置定语,修饰限定先行词"皮影戏"。

3. 译文中添加了"It would be apt to say that",以显示该句是对前文的总结,符合英语的行文习惯。

4. 该句与前文语义重复,译文对其进行了省略。

5. 根据叙述层次,该句在译文中被拆分为两个独立的句子。译文中,对"在13世纪就传到了中东,到了18世纪便有了世界性的影响"采用并列连词and进行衔接,对逻辑关系进行了显化处理,符合英语的行文习惯。

6. 首先,译文对"歌德"及"卓别林"都进行了增译,符合英语的行文习惯,体现了译者的专业性。其次,译文用并列连词and及从属连词when衔接句子,体现了英语重形合的特征。

7. 该句主要介绍皮影戏的产生与发展,根据叙述层次,译文采用并列连词and将两个小句进行衔接,将"中国皮影戏的主要形式此时都具备了"译作由with引导的独立主格结构,对皮影戏的发达程度进行说明。译文语义完整,衔接流畅自然,逻辑层次分明,符合英语的表达习惯。

8. "皮影戏已经相当成熟"概括说明了当时皮影戏的发达程度,"利用皮影戏,就可以演出完整的三国故事等"具体说明了皮影戏在当时的发达程度。英语强调客观具体,且这两部分语义相似,因此译文对"皮影戏已经相当成熟"进行了省略。

9. 译文将"皮影戏是世界上最早由人配音的活动影画艺术"前置于段首进行翻译,将"它的成功给现代电影以很大启发"与"至今皮影戏仍然受到人们的广泛喜爱"通过并列连词and进行连接,使叙述层次更加明晰。

10. 首先,汉语重意合,常有缺省主语的情况出现。英语重形合,主语是基本句型的必备要素。出现原句缺省主语的情况时,可采用语态转换、增加主语等方式处理。译文转换了源语的语态,采用被动语态表达源语内容。其次,根据皮影的具体选材,"皮革"一词应译为"donkey hide",有利于读者更好地理解源语内容,获得与源语读者相同的信息。最后,"颜色鲜艳的人物形象"在译文中用谓语动词进行表达。

11. 首先,根据叙述层次,该句在译文中被拆分为两个独立的句子。其次,"形成活灵活现的剪影"在译文中被处理为whose引导的定语从句,这既符合源语的逻辑关系,又符合译入语的形式要求。再次,译文根据逻辑关系,添加了人称代词 they 作主语，符合英语的结构要求。最后，根据逻辑关系，"若真若幻，赏心悦目"分别被译作现在分词作状语及"which"引导的非限定性定语从句，既符合源语的语言逻辑，又符合目的语的形式要求。

12. 原句中，"站""操纵""演唱"动词连用，译文将"站"译作主句的谓语动词，将"操纵"和"演唱"译作现在分词作伴随状语，并用 while 进行衔接，符合英语的行文习惯。

13. 首先，根据叙述层次，该句被拆分为两个独立的句子。前三个小句逻辑关系较为密切，因此独立成句。剩余内容是对五个人表演皮影戏的分工介绍，因此可译作一个独立的句子。其次，根据逻辑关系，将"陕西华县的皮影戏很有名"译作主句，将"他们形象地称皮影戏为'五人忙'"译作 with 引导的独立主格结构，对主句进行补充说明。"五个人演了一台戏"是皮影戏被称为"五人忙"的原因，因此将其译作原因状语从句。再次，剩余内容介绍五人的具体职责，根据逻辑关系，译文采用分号对其进行衔接。最后，"前声""签手""坐槽""上档""下档"是皮影戏里的行话，在英语文化中没有对应的表达，译文采用音译的策略，以突出这些词的异域文化色彩。

14. 首先，根据叙述层次，将该句译文拆分为两个独立的句子。其次，根据英语的表述习惯，译文对源语的语言顺序进行了调整，将"可不是一件简单的事"置于句首翻译。"演员在幕后手提皮影"指用五根竹棍操纵皮影，因此译文将剩余内容合译为"to operate the puppets using five bamboo sticks"。译文语义内容完整，结构合理，逻辑清晰，符合英义语言规范。根据逻辑关系，"要求演员手指灵活"在译文中增加了代词 it 作主语，指代"to operate the puppets using five bamboo sticks"，既符合源语的语义逻辑，又增强了译文的衔接性。对最后一个小句的衔接，译文采用并列连词 and，符合源语逻辑关系。最后一个小句增译了"with the intriguing movements of the puppets"，使译文形象准确，有利于读者通过文字建构画面，更好地理解中国文化。

参考译文：

Shadow Play: The Art of Light and Shadow

In the latter half of the 18th century, a form of drama arose in France called "French Light and Shadow," which caused a great sensation when it was staged in Paris and Marseilles. This was an artistic form created on the basis of the Chinese shadow play, introduced into France by missionaries. Interestingly, for the 2004 China-France

Year of Culture, Chinese artists introduced to France a new shadow play— *The Dance of Shadows*. It would be apt to say that the art of shadow play has been a witness and bridge to cultural exchange between the two countries.

The shadow play is an indigenous form of drama in China. In the 13th century it was introduced into West Asia, and by the 18th century it had spread to other parts of the world. Famed German poet Goethe (1749–1832) praised it, and the great 20th century artist Charlie Chaplin (1889–1977) was inspired by it when he made his legendary silent films.

The shadow play is in fact the world's earliest "movie art" with the accompaniment of human voice. It first appeared more than 2,000 years ago, and by the Song Dynasty this art had become highly developed with its main artistic form already established. At the time, traditional Chinese drama had not yet developed, but shadow play could already reproduce the entire lengthy story of the Three Kingdoms. It was performed in many cities and became important entertainment at festivals. During the Ming Dynasty, in the city of Beijing alone, there were dozens of shadow play troupes. It is still popular today, and its historical success has given enlightenment to the development of the modern movie.

The making of shadow-play puppets requires choice materials and skills. First, donkey hide has to be found to make the heads, limbs and torsos of the human figures, which are then painted and connected into full puppets using thread and links. During the performance, light shines on the human figures, whose silhouettes are reflected on a screen. Through their movements, they vividly act out stories, creating a world of imagination mixed with reality, which delights both the eyes and hearts of the audience.

The appeal of shadow play lies not only in its puppet-making but more in its performance. Several performers stand behind a white screen, operating puppets of different appearances, while relating the story or singing to the accompaniment of percussions or stringed musical instruments. Shadow plays from Huaxian County of Shaanxi Province are the best known, with local people even giving it another descriptive name as a "Five-person Event," because five performers are involved in each performance. The *qiansheng* is responsible for singing the different roles of a play; the *qianshou* operates the movements of the puppets; the *zuocao* is responsible for beating the gongs, bowls and percussions; the *shangdang* for playing the two-stringed fiddle and trumpet; and the *xiadang* for playing the banhu fiddle and trombone, as well as assisting the *qianshou*. These five people keep busy doing their particular work offstage to put on the performance.

How good a shadow play is depends on the singing and the handling of the puppets. It is no simple matter at all to operate the puppets using five bamboo sticks. It needs deft fingers on the performers' part, and a good puppeteer can dazzle the audience with the intriguing movements of the puppets. （章思英 译）

9. 茶文化

茶是中国的"国饮"。汉字中有一个谜语,谜面是人在草木中,谜底就是茶。唐代(618—907)以前,茶有"荼""槚""荈"等不同名称,唐代以后简化为"茶"字。①

中国是茶的故乡,种茶、饮茶都有悠久的历史。中国人认为茶是炎帝神农发现的。神农是中国远古时代的一位帝王,传说他不但教民播种五谷,而且发明了陶器和炊具。②为了考察对人类有用的植物,神农曾遍尝百草以致中毒,后来发现了茶才得以解毒。③

汉代(前202—公元220)以前,茶主要是作为药物使用的。茶作为饮品的正式记载见于汉代典籍。当时有许多地方开始种茶,并且把茶叶作为商品买卖。魏晋南北朝时期(220—589)饮茶风俗盛行,茶在士大夫阶层及文人雅客的生活中成为待客佳品。到了唐代,饮茶不仅深入到社会各个阶层,而且被人们当作一种艺术活动,这一时期产生了世界上第一部关于茶的专著——陆羽的《茶经》。④这本书系统总结了唐代及以前的制茶工艺及煎茶、饮茶的方法,加深了人们对茶的认识,推动了品茶艺术的发展。⑤

在中国,茶不仅是一种饮料,而且是一种文化。中国很多地方都出产茶叶,茶的种类也很多,如绿茶、红茶、黄茶、白茶、黑茶、花茶、乌龙茶等。一般说来,江浙人爱喝绿茶,东北人爱喝花茶,福建人爱喝乌龙茶。中国有56个民族,受气候、环境和生产生活方式等的影响,一些民族形成了独特的饮茶习俗,如蒙古族的奶茶、藏族的酥油茶等。⑥

中国有"宁可三日无粮,不可一日无茶"的俗话,许多地方都有早晚饮茶的习惯,比如在广东,老年人爱在家喝早茶,年轻人则喜欢去茶楼饮晚茶。⑦饮茶有很多好处:首先可以保健,其次可以娱乐休闲,再者还可以陶冶性情。⑧客来敬茶是中国人的传统,给客人倒茶时不能倒得太满,俗话说:"茶满欺人,酒满敬人。"⑨

中国城乡各地分布着大大小小的茶馆。在北京有一家老舍茶馆,是以中国现代作家老舍及其著名话剧《茶馆》命名的,1988年开业以来已接待了70余位外国领导人、众多社会名流及300多万中外游客,成为展示中国文化的窗口和促进中外友谊的桥梁。⑩(刘谦功、舒燕、于洁《中国文化欣赏读本(上)》)

词汇:

绿茶 green tea

红茶 black tea

黄茶 yellow tea

白茶 white tea

黑茶 dark tea

花茶 scented tea

乌龙茶 oolong

奶茶 milk tea

酥油茶 butter tea

制茶 tea-making

煎茶 tea-baking

饮茶 tea-drinking

翻译解析：

1. 该句由三个小句构成，语义信息可分为两个部分，第一、第二小句说明唐代以前茶的不同名称，第三小句介绍唐代以后茶的名称。鉴于源语的叙述层次及英语的行文习惯，该句被拆分为两个句子进行翻译。

2. 该段的第二句话说明了茶的发明者是神农，第三句话介绍了神农的成就。这两句话存在内在的逻辑关系，因此两个句子可合译为一个句子，以增强译文的逻辑显性，符合英语的行文习惯。

3. 该句由三个部分构成，第一、第二部分说明了神农尝百草的原因及结果，第三部分介绍茶叶能帮助解毒。鉴于源语的叙述层次，译义将该句拆分为两个句子，语言逻辑更加清晰。

4. 该句由四部分构成，第一、第二、第三部分说明了饮茶在唐朝的影响，第四部分则介绍了一个新的信息，即《茶经》这部专著的诞生。译文将此句拆分为两个句子，语义逻辑更加合理。

5. 该句由三部分构成，第一部分是对书的整体介绍，第二、第三部分是书中内容的作用与影响。因此，第二、第三部分在译文中被处理成非限制性定语从句，句子结构更加紧凑。

6. 译者没有将"中国有56个民族"译为"There are 56 ethnic groups in China"，而是译成了"Among the 56 ethnic groups of China"，这样翻译可使之与后文的"一些民族形成了"构成更为合理的逻辑关系。

7. 该句由五部分构成，第一部分介绍了中国的俗话"宁可三日无粮，不可一日无茶"，第二、第三、第四和第五部分则介绍了一些地区的饮茶习惯。因此，可将该句分译成两个句子。

8. 该句由四部分构成,译文同样为四个部分,符合英语的阅读习惯。其中,"饮茶有很多好处"译为"Drinking tea brings people a lot of benefits",补充了其中隐含的"人们"。

9. 该句由三部分构成,按照意群进行划分,第一部分为一个意群,第二、第三部分为一个意群。因此,可将该句拆分成两个句子来译。

10. 该句由四部分构成,第一、第二部分介绍了老舍茶馆的基本信息,第三、第四部分则说明了老舍茶馆的社会影响和作用。译文将该句拆分成两个句子进行翻译,更加符合英语读者的阅读习惯。其中,"成为展示中国文化的窗口和促进中外友谊的桥梁"在翻译时被处理成现在分词短语作伴随状语,这样句子结构更为紧凑。

参考译文:

Tea Culture

Tea is the "national beverage" of China. There is a riddle in the Chinese language saying "a person inside the grass and plant", and the answer is "tea." Before the Tang Dynasty (618-907), tea had a number of different names such as "tu," "jia," "chuan," etc. They were all simplified into "cha" after the Tang Dynasty.

As the homeland of tea, China has a long history of tea-growing and drinking. Chinese people attribute the discovery of tea to Yan Emperor Shennong, a legendary ruler of ancient China who not only taught people cultivation of the five grains but also invented pottery and kitchenware. In his exploration of plants beneficial to human beings, Shennong was poisoned after tasting all the plants. It was not until he found out the detoxification power of tea that he was finally saved.

Before the Han Dynasty (207 BC-AD 220), tea mainly served a medical function. Records of tea as a formal beverage appeared in books of the Han Dynasty when tea was grown in many places and traded as a kind of commodity. During the Northern and Southern dynasties (220-589), the custom of tea drinking prevailed; tea became an ideal product of entertaining guests among the literati and officialdom. With the approach of the Tang Dynasty, tea drinking had not only penetrated all levels of society, but also was regarded by people as a kind of artistic activity. It was during this period that the first monograph on tea, *The Book of Tea* by Lu Yu was written. The book systematically summarized the technique of tea-making and methods of tea-baking and tea-drinking both in and before the Tang Dynasty, which deepened people's understanding of tea and pushed forward the development of the art of tea-savoring.

In China, tea is not only a kind of beverage, but also a form of culture. Tea is produced in many places of China with various kinds, such as green tea, black tea, yellow tea, white tea, dark tea, scented tea and oolong, etc. Generally speaking, people in Jiangsu and Zhejiang provinces like to drink green tea and people from the northeast of China prefer scented tea, while people from Fujian Province like oolong. Among the 56 ethnic groups of China, influenced by distinct climates, environments, ways of production and living, some have developed their own unique tea-drinking customs such as the milk tea of Mongolians and the butter tea of Tibetans and so on.

As a popular saying in China goes, "I'd rather do three days without food, but cannot stand a single day without tea." People in many places keep the habit of drinking tea in the morning and at night. For example, in Guangdong Province, the old people enjoy drinking tea in the morning at home, while young people prefer drinking evening tea in the teahouse. Drinking tea brings people a lot of benefits: in the first place, it's good for the health; in addition, it's a kind of entertainment; moreover, it can also cultivate people's temperament. Serving tea to the guests is a Chinese tradition. The tea cannot be poured too full, because according to the old saying "a full cup of tea is offensive to the guests while a full glass of wine shows respect to them."

Numerous teahouses, no matter big or small, are scattered all over Chinese cities and the countryside. The Lao She Teahouse in Beijing is named after the modern Chinese writer Lao She and his famous play *Teahouse*. Ever since its opening in 1988, it has received more than 70 foreign leaders, multiple socialites as well as over 3,000,000 domestic and foreign tourists, making it a window displaying Chinese culture and a bridge enhancing China's friendship with other countries in the world.(刘谦功、舒燕、于洁《中国文化欣赏读本(上)》)

10. 武术——拳术

　　武术是几千年来中国人强身健体、自卫御敌的方法,也是中国传统的体育项目。武术包括拳术和器械术,拳术是徒手技法的总称,器械术则指手中有武器的武术。

　　俗话说:"天下功夫出少林。"少林武术是中原武术中范围最广、历史最长、种类最多的武术门派,因源于河南嵩山少林寺而得名。①少林拳风格独特,动作刚健有力,擅长技击,在武术界中独树一帜。②

　　少林拳首先要求练好基本功,即站桩。桩有马步桩、椅了桩、丁字桩等,同时也练视、听、抓、拉、推、举、踢等。"拳打一条线"是少林拳最鲜明的特点,法有八要,即起、落、进、退、反、侧、收、纵。③少林拳套路直来直往,动作朴实,几种套路演练均在一条线上,现在少林寺千佛殿上练拳留下的脚窝就是明证。④

　　如果说器械术更带有攻击性的话,那么拳术则更多的是出于健身、防御的目的。有一套拳术叫"五禽戏",由东汉医学家华佗创制,其招式模仿了虎、鹿、熊、猿、鹤五种动物的动作,健身效果为历代养生学家所称赞。⑤

　　中国武术讲究"内练精气神,外练筋骨皮",即把内在精神与外部动作紧密结合起来。⑥精神委顿、劲力不足的人在练拳的时候必是掌无力、眼无神、身不灵、步不稳;反之,练拳不讲究手眼身法步,外形不合规矩,那么精神、气息、力量、功夫也难以练成。⑦当然,"醉拳"是个例外。这种拳打起来很像醉汉酒后摇摇摆摆、跌跌撞撞的样子,但实际上是形醉意不醉,意醉心不醉。⑧其招法——摔打、推拿、跌扑、翻滚、窜蹦、跳跃,既充满了形体艺术的美感,又不失技击实用的特点。

　　中国武术作为一种文化形式,在长期的历史演变中深受中国古代哲学、医学、美学等的影响,如太极拳即接受了道家《易经》的思想。⑨其动作特点是:中正安舒、轻灵圆活、松柔慢匀、开合有序、刚柔相济,如行云流水般连绵不断。⑩这种运动既自然又高雅,有音乐的韵律、哲学的内涵、美术的造型、诗歌的意境,可以全面促进人的身心健康。

　　太极拳也受到了各国人民的欢迎。据不完全统计,仅美国就已有30多种太极拳书籍出版,许多国家还成立了太极拳协会等团体,积极与中国开展交流活动。⑪(刘谦功、舒燕、于洁《中国文化欣赏读本(上)》)

词汇：

武术 martial art

拳术 Chinese boxing

器械术 weapon operations

徒手技法 bare-handed skills

少林拳 Shaolin boxing

站桩 standing on poles

马步桩 horse-riding stance pole

椅子桩 chair-shaped pole

丁字桩 T-shaped pole

五禽戏 five-animal exercise

醉拳 drunken boxing

翻译解析：

1. 该句由两个小句构成，第一个小句说明少林武术的特征，第二小句介绍其名称的由来。鉴于源语的叙述层次及英语的行文便利，该句被拆分为两个句子进行翻译。

2. 该句由四个部分构成，第一、第二、第三部分说明了少林拳的特征，引出了第四部分的"独树一帜"。因此，译文中将第一、第二、第三部分处理成了with引导的伴随状语，使句子的语义逻辑更为清晰。

3. 该句由三个部分构成，按照意群划分，第一部分为第一个意群，第二、第三部分为第二个意群。因此，该句被拆分为两个句子进行翻译，语言逻辑更加清晰。

4. 该句由四部分构成，"几种套路演练均在一条线上"为该句的主句，"套路直来直往，动作朴实"在译文中处理成了主句的伴随状语，"现在少林寺千佛殿上练拳留下的脚窝就是明证"则处理成了定语从句。

5. 该句由四部分构成，其中第一、第二部分为第一个意群，介绍了五禽戏的产生，第三、第四部分为第二个意群，简要说明了五禽戏的动作及其影响。因此，该句在译文中被拆分成了两个句子。

6. 该句由两部分构成，其中"内练精气神，外练筋骨皮"的内练和外练合并译成了"cultivation"，避免了语义的重复。

7. 该句由两个分句组成，在译文中处理成了两个独立的句子。其中，第一个分句中的"掌无力、眼无神、身不灵、步不稳"为四个动词词组，在译文中处理成了四个名词短语"powerless palms, dull eyes, clumsy body and unstable legs"。译文将汉语的动态语言转换成了英语的静态语言，符合英语的表达习惯。

8. 该句由三部分构成，第一、第二部分构成一个意群，第三部分构成一个意群。因此，该句被拆分成两个句子进行翻译。其中，"摇摇摆摆"和"跌跌撞撞"两个叠字短语译为"waddling and blundering"。

9. 该句由三部分构成，按照意群进行划分，第一、第二部分为一个意群，第三部分为一个意群。因此，该句被拆分成两个句子来译。

10. 该句用一系列四字格结构来阐明太极拳的特征，内容形式工整。译文中采用并列的动名词结构进行翻译，保持了形式上的一致性。

11. 该句由四个部分构成，其中第一、第二部分构成一个意群，第三、第四部分构成一个意群。因此，该句被拆分成两个句子进行翻译。

参考译文：

Martial Arts—Chinese Boxing

For thousands of years, martial art has not only been a way for Chinese people to strengthen their bodies and defend themselves, and it is often a traditional Chinese sport. It includes Chinese boxing and weapon operations: the former is the general name for bare-handed skills and the latter is often referred to as armed martial arts.

As the saying goes "martial arts all over China originated in Shaolin Temple." In the Central Plains of China, Shaolin martial art is the most widespread and diverse school of martial arts that enjoys the longest history standing. It is named after Shaolin Temple in the Song Mountain area of Henan Province. With its unique style, vigorous and forceful movements as well as expertise in striking, Shaolin boxing stands apart from other forms of martial arts.

Shaolin boxing requires its learners to master the basics, namely standing on poles, including those for horse-riding stance, chair-shaped, and T-shaped poles, etc. At the same time, watching, listening, grabbing, pulling, pushing, lifting and kicking practices are also executed. "Punching in a straight line" is the most distinctive character of Shaolin boxing. To achieve this principle, eight essentials are required, namely, raising, descending, advancing, retreating, reversing, flanking, withholding, and releasing. Being straightforward with plain actions, the series of skills are performed following the same imaginary line which is clearly evidenced by the deep footprints left during practices in the Thousand Buddha Hall of the Shaolin Temple.

Compared with the more aggressive weapon operation, boxing puts much more emphasis on fitness building and self-defense. There is a set of boxing skills called the "five-animal exercise" which was created by a medical scientist named Hua Tuo in the Eastern Han Dynasty. The exercise imitates actions of five kinds of animals: tigers, deers, bears, apes, and cranes; its fitness-building effect has always received compliments from generations of health preservation scientists.

Chinese martial arts seek the cultivation of internal spirit and external strength which means a close connection of inner spirit and external movements. People who have a poor mental status and lack physical strengths are destined to encounter powerless palms, dull eyes, clumsy body and unstable legs. On the contrary, if the requirements on hands, eyes, body and steps are not met (failure of observing the rules), it would be difficult to master such elements as spirit, breath, strength and technique. Nevertheless, drunken boxing is an exception. Performance of this kind of boxing looks like a drunken man's waddling and blundering. However, the performer is only drunken in appearance but not in mind or consciousness. The skills which include beating, pushing and pulling, tumbling, rolling, leaping and jumping, contains not only the aesthetic sense of physical art but also the practicality of striking techniques.

Chinese martial arts, as a cultural form, are deeply influenced by ancient Chinese philosophy, medical science and aesthetics in the long process of historical development. For instance, taijiquan (tai chi) embraces thoughts from the Taoist classic *The Book of Changes*. Taijiquan has the following features: posing steadily and comfortably, circulating with lightness, stretching and closing with regularity, balancing force and tenderness, moving continuously as floating clouds and flowing water. This kind of sport is both natural and elegant, which possesses the melody of music, philosophical meaning, aesthetic shapes and the imagination of poetry, altogether enhancing people's physical and emotional health from all aspects.

Taijiquan is welcomed by people in every country of the world. According to incomplete statistics, America alone has published more than thirty kinds of books concerning taijiquan. Besides, many countries have set up communities such as taijiquan associations to promote related communication with China. (刘谦功、舒燕、于洁《中国文化欣赏读本(上)》)

11. 书法

中国书法驰名世界,我们可以从性质、渊源、美学特征、表现手法等方面来欣赏中国书法,它体现了万事万物"对立统一"的基本规律,也反映了人作为万物之灵的精神与气质。①

随着汉字的变化,中国书法也在变化,出现了各种书体,主要有五种。

第一,篆书。一般指小篆,是秦始皇统一文字所用的书体,汉代(公元前206年—公元220年)沿用,文字已规范化,偏旁有固定的形式和位置,空虚之处尽量用笔画填满。②

第二,隶书。产生于战国(公元前475年—公元前221年),盛行于汉代,打破了篆书曲屈圆转的形体结构,笔画比较平直,魏晋(公元220年—公元420年)以后隶书的正统地位被楷书取代,多用于匾额、碑石。③

第三,楷书。字形方正,是在汉末八分书的基础上演变而成的新书体,三国(公元220年—公元280年)时通行全国,隋唐(公元581年—公元907年)以后在书法风格上有了新的发展,代表作有唐代颜真卿的《多宝塔碑》、元代赵孟頫的《福神观记》等。楷书一直作为正体字沿用至今。④

第四,草书。草书的特点是笔画相连,书写迅捷,初成于汉代,是为求简便在隶书的基础上产生的。草书笔势流畅、风格潇洒,极具艺术性和美感,代表作如唐代怀素的《自叙帖》、清代邓石如的《五言诗轴》等。⑤

第五,行书。行书指介于正体字和草书之间的流畅书体,既便于书写,又不像草书那样难于辨认。⑥从汉代起,行书随着正体字的发展在体势、笔意上有所变化,成为适应性最强、应用范围最广、延续时间最长的书体。行书代表作以晋代王羲之的《兰亭序》、宋代苏东坡的《黄州寒食诗帖》最为著名。⑦

中国书法作为艺术始于春秋战国,成熟于秦汉,在魏晋南北朝时达到炉火纯青的境界,人们将"汉赋、晋字、唐诗、宋词、元曲"相提并论,足见晋字成就之高。⑧书圣王羲之便生于这个时代,关于他还流传着一个有趣的故事:王羲之注重师法自然,他说鹅是"禽中豪杰,白如雪,洁如玉,一尘不染",便喜欢观察鹅的动态以揣摩自己的运笔。⑨一天清晨,王羲之乘船观赏山水,不觉对岸边一群白鹅看得出神,便想买回去,鹅的主人是一位道士,他说:"倘若大人想要,就请给我写一部道家养生修炼的《黄庭经》吧!"⑩王羲之求鹅心切,便应允了,用他的书法换了白鹅。

时至今日,中国人依然热爱着书法,使用着书法。古老的书法不仅魅力不减,而且吸引着许许多多的外国人,无论是中国汉语国际教育的课堂,还是海外孔子学院的文化活动,都离不开书法的展示、讲解与练习,现在书法已成为中外文化交流的一种重要媒介。⑪(刘谦功、舒燕、于洁《中国文化欣赏读本(下)》)

词汇:

书法 calligraphy

汉字 Chinese characters

篆书 the seal script

小篆 small seal character

隶书 the official script

楷书 the regular script

草书 the cursive script

行书 the running script

偏旁 Chinese character components

体势 character form

笔意 calligraphic style

翻译解析:

1. 该句由四个小句构成,语义信息可分为两个部分。第一、第二个小句说明中国书法的鉴赏方法,第三、第四个小句介绍了中国书法的内在特征。鉴于源语的叙述层次及英语的行文便利,译文将该句拆分为两个句子进行翻译。

2. 该句由六个小句构成,按照语义可以划分为三个意群。第一、第二小句为第一个意群,简要说明了篆书的产生。第三、第四小句是第二个意群,说明了篆书在汉代的使用。第五、第六小句是第三个意群,说明了汉字在汉代的书写方式。因此,译文将该句拆分成三个句子进行翻译,语义逻辑更为清晰。

3. 该句由六个小句构成。按照意群划分,第一至第四小句为第一个意群,第五、第六小句为第二个意群。因此,将该句拆分为两个句子进行翻译,语言逻辑更加清晰。

4. 该句由六个小句构成,按照意群划分,第一、第二小句为第一个意群,简要说明了楷书的形成。第三、第四小句为第二个意群,介绍了楷书的应用和发展。第五小句是第三个意群,列举了楷书的代表作。第六小句是第四个意群,说明了楷书的影响。因此,将该句拆分为四个句子进行翻译,语言逻辑更加清晰。

5. 该句由四部分构成,其中第一、第二部分为第一个意群,介绍了草书的特征。第三、第四部分为第二个意群,介绍了草书的代表作。因此,该句在译文中被拆分成了两个句子。

6. 该句由三部分构成,其中第一部分为第一个意群,简要说明了行书是介于正体字和草书之间的一种书体。第二、第三部分为第二个意群,介绍了行书的特征。因此,该句在译文中被拆分成了两个句子。

7. 该句由四个部分组成,按照意群划分,第一、第二部分为第一个意群,简要说明了行书的变化。第三部分为第二个意群,介绍了行书的应用和影响。第四部分是第三个意群,列举了行书的代表作。因此,将该句拆分成三个句子进行翻译,语义逻辑更为清晰。

8. 该句由四部分构成,第一、第二部分构成一个意群,第三、第四部分构成一个意群。因此,将该句拆分成两个句子进行翻译。

9. 该句由五部分构成,按照意群进行划分,第一部分为一个意群,简要介绍了王羲之。第二、第三、第四部分为一个意群,第五部分为一个意群。因此,将该句拆分成了三个句子来译。

10. 该句由五部分构成,按照意群进行划分,第一、第二、第三部分为一个意群,介绍了王羲之乘船观赏山水发现白鹅的经历。第四、第五部分为一个意群,讲鹅主人对王羲之说的话。因此,将该句拆分成了两个句子来翻译。

11. 该句由六个部分构成,其中第一、第二部分构成一个意群,第三、第四、第五部分构成一个意群,第六部分构成一个意群。因此,将该句拆分成三个句子进行翻译。其中第二个意群的翻译进行了主语的转换,将原文的主语"中国汉语国际教育的课堂"和"海外孔子学院的文化活动"转换成了"书法的展示、讲解与练习",即"Calligraphy display, explanation and practice",语态由主动变为被动,更符合英语的表达习惯。

参考译文:

Chinese Calligraphy

The world-famous Chinese calligraphy can be appreciated from its nature, origin, aesthetic features, and performance characteristics. It reveals the basic law of unity of the opposites in the universe and reflects the spirit and temperament of human beings as the wisest of all creatures.

Along with the changes of Chinese characters, Chinese calligraphy also underwent some changes and different calligraphic styles came into existence. There are five main categories.

First, the seal script. Generally referring to small seal characters, they were adopted by the First Emperor of the Qin Dynasty with the purpose of standardizing the script. It was still used in the Han Dynasty (206 BC–AD 220) when characters were already standardized. At that time, the Chinese character components had fixed form and place, and the blank space was filled with strokes as much as possible.

Second, the official script. Originating from the Warring States Period (475 BC–221 BC) and prevailing in the Han Dynasty, it is straight in the line strokes, which is different from the curved shape of the seal script. After the Wei and Jin dynasties (220–420) when regular script replaced official script as the legitimate character style, official script was often used in horizontal inscribed boards and steles.

Third, the regular script. Square in shape, it is a new calligraphic style evolving from *ba fen* style at the end of the Han Dynasty. It prevailed all around the country in the Three Kingdoms (220–280) and underwent new developments in calligraphic style in the Sui and Tang dynasties (581–907). The masterpieces include *Multi-pagoda Stele* by Yan Zhenqing of the Tang Dynasty and *Note of Fushen Temple* by Zhao Mengfu of the Yuan Dynasty. Regular script is still in use today as the standard character writing format.

Fourth, the cursive script. It appears in the Han Dynasty on the basis of seal script for convenience, featuring letters that are joined in a rapid flowing style. Cursive script is extremely artistic and beautiful with its fluent handwriting and natural style. The master works include *Autobiography* by Huai Su in the Tang Dynasty and *Scroll of Poems with Five Characters to a Line* by Deng Shiru in the Qing Dynasty.

Fifth, the running script. It refers to the flowing calligraphic style between *zhengti* characters and cursive script. It is easy to write and not as difficult to recognize as cursive script. Since the Han Dynasty, running script has undergone some changes in character forms and calligraphic styles with the development of *zhengti* characters. It became the most well-adapted calligraphic style with the widest range of applications as well as the longest duration. Among the works of running script, the most well-known ones are the *Preface of the Orchid Pavilion* by Wang Xizhi in the Jin Dynasty and *Poem Written during the Cold Food Festival in Huangzhou* by Su Shi in the Song Dynasty.

As a form of art, Chinese calligraphy began in the Spring and Autumn Period and the Warring States Period and matured in the Qin and Han dynasties and reached high perfection in the Wei, Jin, Northern and Southern dynasties. The great achievement of calligraphy in the Jin Dynasty is obvious because articles of the Han Dynasty, calligraphy of the Jin Dynasty, poetry of the Tang Dynasty, *ci* of the Song Dynasty and *qu* of the Yuan Dynasty are always mentioned in the same breath. Wang Xizhi, known as "the saint of calligraphy," lived in this age. An interesting story goes like this: Wang Xizhi stressed getting inspiration from nature and said that goose "is the hero of poultry because it is spotless, as white as snow and as clean as jade." Therefore, he loved to observe the movements of goose to think about how to wield his writing brush. One morning when Wang enjoyed the landscape scenery on boat top, he was unconsciously absorbed in was a Taoist priest who said that "if you want to get the geese, please write for me *The Yellow Court Classic* as for Taoists to keep in good health!" Wang Xizhi was so desperate to get the geese that he agreed and exchanged his calligraphy for the white geese.

Even to this day, Chinese people still love and use calligraphy. The old calligraphy does not lose its charm but attracts many foreigners. Calligraphy display, explanation and practice are seen both in international education courses of Chinese characters and in cultural events in Confucius Institutes overseas. Nowadays calligraphy has become an important medium of cultural communication between China and other countries.（刘谦功、舒燕、于洁《中国文化欣赏读本（下）》）

12. 长城

长城蜿蜒万里,东端是山海关,西端是嘉峪关。山海关临渤海,位于河北省秦皇岛市东北15公里处,有"天下第一关"之称,四座主要城门与多种防御建筑巍然而立。①嘉峪关在嘉峪山上,位于甘肃省嘉峪关市西面5公里处,是古代丝绸之路的交通要冲,由内城、外城、城壕三道防线构成重叠并守之势。②山海关与嘉峪关遥相呼应,与其间数不清的关隘共同托起了万里长城。

长城是中国古代在不同时期为抵御塞北游牧部落联盟侵袭而修筑的规模浩大的军事工程,东西绵延上万华里,因此被称为"万里长城"。③长城始建于春秋战国时代,现存的长城遗址主要为14世纪的明长城。④国家文物局2009年公布,中国明长城总长度为8851.8千米。长城是中国古代劳动人民创造的伟大奇迹,是中国悠久历史的见证。

春秋战国时期,各国诸侯为了防御别国入侵修筑烽火台,并用城墙将诸多烽火台连接起来,形成了最早的长城。⑤此后历代君王几乎都加固增修长城。据记载,秦始皇使用了近百万劳动力修筑长城,占全国总人口的二十分之一。当时没有任何机械设备,一切都由人力完成,工作环境又是崇山峻岭,十分艰难。当时的人绝没有想到,这长城一修就是数千年、上万里,难怪古今中外,凡是到过长城的人都会惊叹它宏伟的规模、磅礴的气势,长城也因此成为文学艺术永恒的主题。⑥

居庸关位于北京,有"天下第一雄关"之称,这里两山对峙,一水中流,山上城墙蜿蜒,山下城楼巍峨。⑦关城内庙宇、署馆、亭坊、仓房层叠错落,红墙、碧瓦、彩画相映生辉。关城以险峻著称,有"一夫当关,万夫莫开"之势。居庸关不仅地势险要,而且风景宜人。⑧历代文人墨客在此留下了许多赞咏的诗篇,乾隆皇帝也在此御笔亲提"居庸叠翠"四字,成为著名的"燕山八景"之一。⑨

雁门关位于山西,东有雁门山,西靠隆山,每年大雁于其间南来北往,故称雁门。⑩雁门关关城周长二里,墙高一丈八尺,有三座门。东门之上筑有楼台,名曰雁楼,有"天险"石匾;西门之上筑有杨六郎庙,有"地利"石匾。北门未建楼台,门额上书"雁门关"三个大字,左右有对联一副:"三关冲要无双地,九寨尊崇第一关。"

长城的伟大与壮观有目共睹,世人皆知,它永远是中华民族的骄傲。⑪(刘谦功、舒燕、于洁《中国文化欣赏读本(下)》)

词汇：

长城 the Great Wall

山海关 Shanhaiguan Pass

嘉峪关 Jiayuguan Pass

游牧部落 nomadic tribes

军事工程 military project

烽火台 beacon tower

秦始皇 the First Emperor of Qin

居庸关 Juyongguan Pass

署馆 office bureaus

亭坊 pavilion

仓房 storehouse

文人墨客 literati and poets

雁门关 Yanmenguan Pass

石匾 plaque

翻译解析：

1. 该句由四个部分构成,语义信息可分为两个部分,第一、第二、第三个小句说明了长城的地理位置和美誉,第四个小句简要介绍了城门和防御建筑。鉴于源语的叙述层次,该句被拆分为两个句子进行翻译。

2. 该句由四个部分构成,按照语义可以划分为两个意群。第一、第二部分为第一个意群,简要说明了嘉峪关所处的地理位置。第三、第四部分是第二个意群,说明了嘉峪关在丝绸之路上的重要性。因此,将该句拆分成两个句子进行翻译,语义逻辑更为清晰。

3. 该句由三个部分构成。按照意群划分,第一、第二部分为第一个意群,说明了长城的军事重要性。第三部分为第二个意群,说明了长城的长度。因此,将该句拆分为两个句子进行翻译,语言逻辑更加清晰。

4. 该句由两个部分构成。按照意群划分,第一部分为第一个意群,简要说明了长城的始建时间。第二部分为第二个意群,介绍了现存长城遗址。因此,将该句拆分为两个句子进行翻译,语言逻辑更加清晰。

5. 该句由四部分构成,其中第一、第二、第三部分介绍了长城的形成过程。第四部分为前三部分的结果。因此,第四部分在译文中处理成了非谓语动词短语作结果状语,句子结构更为紧凑。

6. 该句由五部分构成,其中第一、第二部分为第一个意群,第三、四部分为第二个意群,第五部分为第三个意群。因此,该句在译文中被拆分成了三个句子。

7. 该句由六个部分组成。按照意群划分,第一、第二部分为第一个意群,简要说明了居庸关的地理位置。第三、第四部分为第二个意群,介绍了居庸关的地理优势。第五、第六部分是第三个意群,介绍了居庸关的地理特征。因此,将该句拆分成三个句子进行翻译,语义逻辑更为清晰。

8. 该句中的"地势险要"和"风景宜人"为两个四字格的形容词,在英语中很难找到意思和形式与其对等的形容词。因此,在译文中分别将其译为动词短语"has a terrain of great strategic importance"和"possesses pleasant scenery"。

9. 该句由三部分构成。按照意群进行划分,第一部分为一个意群,简要说明了居庸关备受文人墨客赞咏。第二、第三部分为一个意群,介绍了乾隆皇帝的题字。因此,将该句拆分为两个句子进行翻译,语言逻辑更加清晰。

10. 该句由五部分构成。按照意群进行划分,第一、第二、第三部分为一个意群,介绍了雁门关的地理位置。第四、第五部分为一个意群,说明了"雁门"的来历。因此,译文将该句拆分成两个句子来翻译。

11. 该句由三个部分构成,其中第一、第二部分构成一个意群,第三部分构成一个意群。因此,将该句拆分成两个句子进行翻译。

参考译文:

The Great Wall

Meandering for tens of thousands of miles, the Great Wall begins in the east at Shanhaiguan Pass and ends at Jiayuguan Pass in the west. Facing the Bohai Sea, Shanhaiguan Pass is situated 15 kilometers northeast of Qinhuangdao City in Hebei Province and is regarded as "the number one pass in the world." Its four main gates, together with various kinds of defensive structures, stand in majestic splendor. Jiayuguan Pass lies on Jiayu Mountain 5 kilometers west of Jiayuguan City in Gansu Province. It once served as a transport hub for the ancient Silk Road. Its three lines of defense, including the inner city, outer city and city moat, form an overlapping fortification system. Echoing each other at great distance, Shanhaiguan Pass and Jiayuguan Pass collaboratively form the "ten-thousand *li* Great Wall" with the numerous passes embedded in between.

The Great Wall is a massive military project that was built in different periods of ancient China to prevent intrusions by allies of nomadic tribes in the north. Stretching for tens of thousands of *li* from east to west, the ancient fortification derived its name the "ten-thousand *li* Great Wall." Construction of the Great Wall started in the Spring and Autumn and the Warring States periods. The majority of the existing walls belong to the 14th century Ming Dynasty walls. According to the announcement made by the State Administration of Cultural Heritage, the Ming Dynasty Great Wall measures 8,851.8 km. As a great wonder created by ancient Chinese people, the Great Wall witnessed the long history of China.

In the Spring and Autumn and the Warring States periods, in order to prevent external invasions, rulers of each state constructed beacon towers and connected them by walls, resulting in the earliest form of the Great Wall. Almost all the subsequent rulers had reinforced or extended the Great Wall. According to the records, the First Emperor of Qin exploited almost one million laborers in the construction of the Great Wall, making up one twentieth of the Qin Dynasty's population. The construction was an arduous task, for no machines existed then, and all work was finished by laborers working in an environment full of high mountains and lofty hills. People living in that period probably had never anticipated that the construction of the wall was to last for thousands of years and reach thousands of miles. It is no wonder that people who have been to the Great Wall, regardless of the time and their nationalities, will invariably be impressed by its massive scale and majesty. Therefore, the Great Wall came to establish itself as an eternal theme in literature and art.

Located in Beijing, Juyongguan Pass is referred to as "the most majestic pass in the world." Here, two mountains stand facing each other with a river flowing in between. The top of the mountain is lined with meandering walls, and the mountain foot is full of city towers soaring up to the sky. Inside the city at Juyongguan Pass, temples, office bureaus, pavilions and storehouses are scattered around; the red walls, glazed tiles and colorful paintings set each other off to form a brilliant scene. The exterior of the city is renowned for its precipitousness characterized by the saying one man guarding the pass will prevent 10,000 enemies from getting through." Juyongguan Pass not only has a terrain of great strategic importance, but also possesses pleasant scenery. Generations of literati and poets had left behind numerous poems praising the natural beauty of the site. The inscriptions of Emperor Qianlong's words "居庸叠翠"(the lush green at Juyongguan Pass) helped it to become one of the famous "eight scenic spots" in Beijing.

Rising up in Shanxi Province, Yanmenguan Pass is sided by Yanmen Mountain in the east and Longshan Mountain in the west. Wild geese migrate back and forth between northern and southern China via Yanmenguan Pass, hence the name Yanmenguan (wild geese gate). With a perimeter of one kilometer, the city at Yanmenguan Pass is fortified by walls measuring six meters high and it contains three gates. A tower called Yanlou (wild geese tower) was constructed on the wall above the east gate, with a plaque bearing the word "天险"(natural barrier). The west gate fortress is a temple accommodating the Shrine of Yang Yanzhao (a military general in the Song Dynasty), with a plaque bearing "地利"(topographical advantages). No towers were constructed on the north gate, instead three bold characters "雁门关"(Yanmenguan Pass) are inscribed on the lintel of the gate. On the left and right sides of the gate, there is a couplet saying "三关冲要无双地,九寨尊崇第一关"(No place matches Yanmenguan Pass in importance, the pass is honored as the top among all the nine passes).

The grandeur and magnificence of the Great Wall is universally acknowledged and recognized. It will always be the pride of Chinese people. (刘谦功、舒燕、于洁《中国文化欣赏读本(下)》)

参考文献

包惠南. 中国文化与汉英翻译[M]. 北京:外文出版社,2004.

曹雪芹. 红楼梦[M]. 杨宪益,戴乃迭,译. 北京:外文出版社,1994.

陈宏薇. 新实用汉译英教程[M]. 武汉:湖北教育出版社,1996.

陈宏薇. 高级汉英翻译[M]. 北京:外语教学与研究出版社,2009.

陈宏薇,李亚丹. 新编汉英翻译教程[M]. 上海:上海外语教育出版社,2013.

陈建平. 翻译与跨文化交际[M]. 北京:外语教学与研究出版社,2012.

陈毅平,秦学信. 大学英语文化翻译教程[M]. 北京:外语教学与研究出版社,2014.

冯庆华. 实用翻译教程[M]. 上海:上海外语教育出版社,2010.

傅景华. 黄帝内经素问译注[M]. 北京:中国人民大学出版社,2010.

国务院新闻办公室. 新时代中国青年[EB/OL]. [2022－04－21]. http://language.chinadaily.com.cn/a/202204/21/WS62611ee0a310fd2b29e58788.html.

国务院新闻办公室. 中国的粮食安全[EB/OL]. [2019－10－15]. https://language.chinadaily.com.cn/a/201910/15/WS5da55f04a310cf3c55570946.html.

国务院新闻办公室. 元宵节的起源[EB/OL]. [2014－02－14]. https://language.chinadaily.com.cn/a/201402/14/WS5b2070e6a31001b82572029b.html.

国家主席习近平发表二○一八年新年贺词. [EB/OL]. [2018－01－05]. http://www.china.org.cn/chinese/2018－01／05/content_50195196.htm.

决胜全面建成小康社会夺取新时代中国特色社会主义伟大胜利:在中国共产党第十九次全国代表大会上的报告. [EB/OL]. [2017－11－06]. http://language.chinadaily.com.cn/19thcpcnationalcongress/2017 11/06/content_34188086_5.htm.

贾雨新. 跨文化交际学[M]. 上海:上海外语教育出版社,1998.

兰萍. 英汉文化互译教程[M]. 北京:中国人民大学出版社,2010.

老舍. 骆驼祥子[M]. 施晓菁,译. 北京:外文出版社,2001.

李定坤. 汉英辞格对比与翻译[M]. 武汉:华中师范大学出版社,1994.

李申. 汉民族语言审美心理与翻译审美的关系[J]. 山东外语教学,1998,(04):55－59.

李玉良,罗公利. 儒家思想在西方的翻译与传播[M]. 北京:中国社会科学出版社,2009.

吕叔湘. 翻译工作与"杂学"[M]// 罗新璋. 翻译论集. 北京:商务印书馆,2009.

刘宓庆. 文化翻译论纲[M]. 北京：中译出版社,2016.

刘宓庆. 新编汉英对比与翻译[M]. 北京：中国对外翻译出版公司,2010.

刘谦功,舒燕,于洁. 中国文化欣赏读本[M]. 北京：北京语言大学出版社,2014.

刘瑞琴,韩淑芹,张红. 英汉委婉语对比与翻译[M]. 银川：宁夏人民出版社,2010.

卢红梅. 华夏文化与汉英翻译[M]. 武汉：武汉大学出版社,2006.

鲁迅. 阿Q正传[M]. 杨宪益,戴乃迭,译. 北京：外文出版社,2001.

鲁迅. 朝花夕拾[M]. 杨宪益,戴乃迭,译. 北京：外文出版社,2000.

莫言. 生死疲劳[M]. 北京：作家出版社,2012.

奈达. 语言与文化[M]. 上海：上海外语教育出版社,2001.

乔萍,瞿淑蓉,宋洪玮. 散文佳作108篇[M]. 南京：译林出版社,2010.

泰勒. 原始文化 神话、哲学、宗教、语言、艺术和习俗发展之研究[M]. 连树声,译. 南宁：广西师范大学出版社,2005.

王嵘. 解读"黑色"的中西方文化差异[J]. 文化学刊,2009,(1)：136-139.

吴敬梓. 儒林外史[M]. 杨宪益,戴乃迭,译. 长沙：湖南出版社,1996.

谢天振. 中西翻译简史[M]. 北京：外语教学与研究出版社,2009.

许钧. 文学翻译批评研究[M]. 南京：译林出版社,2012.

杨平. 名作精译[M]. 青岛：青岛出版社,1998.

叶朗,朱良志. 中国文化读本[M]. 北京：外语教学与研究出版社,2008a.

叶朗,朱良志. Insights into Chinese culture[M]. 章思英,陈海燕,译. 北京：外语教学与研究出版社,2008b.

叶子南. 高级英汉翻译理论与实践[M]. 北京：北京清华大学出版社,2013.

余雯蔚,周武忠. 五色观与中国传统用色现象[J]. 艺术百家,2007(05)：138-140.

张拱贵. 汉语委婉语词典[M]. 北京：北京语言文化大学出版社,1996.

张培基. 英译中国现代散文选(一)[M]. 上海：上海外语教育出版社,2007.

张润晗,王素娥,霍盛亚. 英汉语言对比与互译[M]. 北京：清华大学出版社,2018.

中国社会科学院语言研究所词典编辑室. 现代汉语词典：2002年增补本[Z]. 北京：商务印书馆,2002.

庄绎传. 英汉翻译简明教程[M]. 北京：外语教学与研究出版社,2002.

祖林. "白色"在英汉语中的内涵对比研究[J]. 文化论坛,2011,(4)：161.

EUGEGE A N. Toward a science of translating [M]. Shanghai：Shanghai Foreign Language Education Press, 2004a.

EUGENE A N, TABER C R. The theory and practice of translation [M]. ShanGhai：Shanahai Foreign Language Education Press, 2004b.

GOIDBIATT. Life and death are wearing me out [M]. New York: Arcade Publishing, 2008.

KELLY J, MAO N K. Fortress Besieged [M]. Beijing: Foreign Language Teaching and Research Press, 2003.

NI M. The yellow emperors classic of medicine[M]. Berkeley: Shambhala, 1995.